my business
my success

A Woman's Guide to Entrepreneurship

Edited by Helen Jamieson

© Copyright Helen Jamieson 2013

Published by:
Jaluch Limited, Jaluch House, Deweys Lane, Ringwood, Hants
BH24 1AJ, UK.

First edition.

Visit us at: http://www.jaluch.co.uk

T: +44(0)1425 479888   E: help@jaluch.co.uk

Author: Helen Jamieson

Design and layout: Elizabeth McDonald

All rights reserved. No part of this work may be reproduced, stored in a retrieval system, or transmitted in any form or by any means, electronic, mechanical photocopying, recording, or otherwise, without prior permission of the copyright owner.

ACKNOWLEDGEMENTS

It might be an odd place to start, but this book would not be here today were it not for all those people who suggested I couldn't do it, or shouldn't do it, or who just gave me those odd looks of bewilderment that I even wanted to do it! I am very grateful to them for my current determination to succeed!

There have been many, though, who have supported me along the way and, in particular, in writing this book. Specifically I want to thank my gorgeous, intelligent daughter, Suzie, who is always so incredibly supportive, loyal and encouraging. I also want to thank Sally Bailey for her constant loyalty and support and for having the courage to so often challenge my thinking, when others would just let me head up the wrong path. Tina Thomson too has been an absolute inspiration since I met her in 2012. She is the role model that all women need to find and learn from and her support and enthusiasm have blown me away at times. David Clutterbuck might not know it, but he has over the past year given me balance and perspective and I just love his enthusiasm for everything he does in life. An amazing person to bring energy into the room. And last but not least Patrick who, perhaps unwittingly at times, has taught me so much in recent years about myself and where my strengths lie. Patrick also gave me the idea for the title for this book!

One group that has continually inspired me has been my Women Presidents' Organisation group. I joined the WPO around four years ago and we meet in London once a month for three hours. Every single month I learn things, and without all that learning and sharing of ideas and experiences over the past few years this book would not be here today.

I also want to thank all of those who have contributed to this book: Elaine Strydom in South Africa; Alicia Carballo in Argentina; Julie Weeks in the US; Amanda Pelham Green, Linda Rowe and Christine Asiko in the UK; Madeleine van der Steege in the Netherlands; Sarah Steel in the UK; Robyn Heathfield in South Africa; Carrie Beddingfield, Gill Thorpe, Sherry Moran, Karen Emanuel and Scott Dougan, all in the UK. And also all those who so generously gave their time by reading chapters for me and giving me their feedback and ideas.

Then finally there are all my anonymous supporters who completed my online survey when I was trying to decide a title for this book. Thank you all for your comments and ideas about what you liked, disliked and what is important to you and if I didn't choose the title you most preferred, please accept my humble apologies and know that in many respects it was a close-run race!

FOREWORD
by professor david clutterbuck

One of my many heroes is Dame Steve Shirley, for whose company FI (as it was then) I became a sort of unofficial historian, capturing the essence of the culture at several points in its early history. One of the many lessons I learned was that the extra measure of tenacity it took for a determined woman to set up a substantial business, while it might have been painful at the time, was a hugely positive shaping influence on the business and its leadership.

I see this same phenomenon many times over, in mentoring programmes that target female entrepreneurs, such as that from the Cherie Blair Foundation. Yes, it is in most societies more difficult for a woman to set up and grow a business than for a man. But for a variety of reasons – many of them related to the learning that comes from overcoming barriers – those businesses tend to be more robust, with a greater than average survivability. At a microbusiness level in developing countries, they also tend to contribute more to the local economy.

One of the many things I like about this very practical book is how it tackles the common barriers so many women experience in setting up in business. Of these, the one I encounter most often is lack of self-belief – the sense that she lacks the skills, the knowledge, the personal resourcefulness to be a successful entrepreneur. Even if it were true (and it rarely is) anyone with a reasonable level of commercial instinct can create a viable business, if they start with their strengths and work out how to buy in (or get for free) the expertise to compensate for their weaknesses.

Other barriers I observe include:

- ❖ A passive acceptance that the leadership style and practices of businesses designed and run by men are the only way (or the only right way) to lead. Many of the most successful entrepreneurs I have met have extracted themselves from such organisations, determined to create enterprises that reflect their own values and leadership style. In most cases, they have created great places to work. By contrast, women, who have transferred into their businesses the kind of leadership they have been subjected to as employees, tend to have lower employee engagement and overall tend to be less successful long-term.

- ❖ Shortness of vision. Analysis by INSEAD of the leadership competencies of its alumni found that on average women outscored men on most of the characteristics measured – the one exception being strategic visioning. Whereas men often think unrealistically big, female entrepreneurs may tend to think too small. It is an old, but useful, axiom that, if you go to a bank and ask for £5,000, your proposal is likely to receive greater and more critical scrutiny than if you ask for £100,000.

- ❖ Lack of support from family and friends. Self-belief is powerful, but self-belief coupled with the belief of others is far more so. If you haven't got a strong support network at home, go and find one. Having a mentor (or better, several mentors) is one common way to develop this kind of resource. Intriguingly, successful men often make better mentors of women than their female counterparts, perhaps because they do not feel in competition.

These observations, I hasten to add, are not the result of empirical research, but of working with and listening to a wide variety of entrepreneurial women over many years. When I discuss these observations with female audiences, however, there is usually a high level of agreement that these are real issues.

In recent years, there has been a lot of media and government attention to the need to achieve a greater balance between men and women on company boards. One of the reasons progress is so slow, I believe, is that there have been relatively few exemplars of female entrepreneurs, who know what it's like to build a substantial business from scratch. That's changing and I hope this book will assist in making that change happen even faster!

ABOUT
professor david clutterbuck

I am very grateful to David for writing the foreword for this book. David has been enormously supportive of me over the past year and I love his style and his energy. His humour too, but that can take a bit of getting used to at times!

David pioneered the development, embedding and sustainability of coaching and mentoring cultures in the workplace and remains the foremost international thought leader in this powerful area of development. He co-founded the European Mentoring & Coaching Council and is now Special Ambassador for the EMCC.

David has been described as one of the world's most thought-provoking and entertaining speakers and writers on management and human resources, and as an iconoclast with a wicked sense of humour and a relentless pursuit of evidence about what does and doesn't work. He describes himself as a serial entrepreneur and as an adventurer.

David himself is a prolific author, with fifty-five books at the last count, including one book of comic children's stories. He is also Visiting Professor at Sheffield Hallam & Oxford Brookes universities and an external examiner for the Ashridge Coaching MBA. As he says of himself, 'Everything I do revolves around helping people and organisations harness the power of dialogue.'

is this book for you?

my ideas for setting up in business, running a business and succeeding in business.

In this book I want to share with you my ideas for setting up in business, running a business and succeeding in business.

This book is not for Alpha Females who were born knowing that they can beat every man and woman they ever meet hands down. Who were born with confidence levels and self-esteem that the rest of us are in awe of. It is also not for those who have picked up this book saying to themselves, 'I already know it all and what can anyone teach me.'

But it is also not for the faint-hearted, those who have a tendency to pessimism, and those who think that self-employment is likely to be a cushier number than employment – lazy people don't make great entrepreneurs.

Rather, this book is for those women who have a dream to set up in business, but who perhaps don't know where to start. And those women who are just in the process of setting up, but who want to know how to do it well and avoid some of the pitfalls along the way. And those women who are already running businesses, but who are seeking a few new ideas, inspiration or support.

It's a book for those who want to learn and to achieve. A book for those who aspire to financial independence. For those who want to use their brains, stretch themselves and travel on new journeys. And perhaps, most importantly for me, this book is for those who want to help change the world for their daughters.

When I was in my late twenties and still employed I started to think about setting up a business. I bought a couple of (very dry and lacklustre) books on setting up your own business and read them during my lunch hours, sat in the company car park escaping just temporarily from a job and company I really didn't enjoy.

It was lovely to read and plan and dream about the future even if my head was full of thoughts of … how can I make this happen, what if I fail, what company can I set up, how will I know what to do, is this just a dream or can I make it a reality?

But I did make it happen and you can too. In fact from reading those books to setting up my first venture it only took a year or so – helped by a boot up the backside from an employer who didn't really want me anymore as I'd just had a baby.

There is no particular right way or wrong way to set up and run a business. There is no right or wrong personality type to run a successful business. And there is often no right or wrong time of life to set up in business. Therefore, in essence there is no reason why anyone cannot give running their own business a go … and succeed.

But my first question to you is: how much do you want to be your own boss? How much do you want to set up a successful enterprise?

Be honest with yourself because you have got to want this a lot for it to be worth the effort you are about to put in. I really hope, though, you decide that you want this as much as I did all those years ago!

There are currently 104 million women worldwide who own their own businesses. I am proud to be one of them. I would also love you to become one of our group and perhaps one day soon we will be able to say there are 200 million of us. Now that will make an incredible community of business women!

CONTENTS

#1 ambition 17

A little thinking about ambition

What motivates you?

Self-employed or an entrepreneur?

#2 thinking things through 31

What do you want?

A little about profit margins

A business for your retirement

A business with young children

A business because no one else will give you a job!

What are you going to sell?

Assessing if your business idea will fly

Exit strategies to decide before you even get going

#3 how much will you risk? 63

#4 what's in a name? 69

#5 branding 73

Creating your business brand

Values

Product branding

Creating a personal brand

#6　business planning　　89

Why plan and why do so few have a plan?

What goes into the business plan

Succeeding in business

#7　running your business　　99

The tedious admin

Outsourcing the jobs you don't know how to do

Employing and managing staff

Innovating in business

Business vampires

#8　sales　　137

Your elevator pitch

What sort of salesperson are you?

Offering incentives

Negotiating

Low-hanging fruit

Sales mistakes

#9　finance　　161

Cash flow

Keeping good accounts

Cash and how it can impact on your accounting

Time is money

Fraud

Setting up on a shoestring

#10　focus on you! 183

Your supporters – how supportive are they really?

Growing your business and growing your skills

Developing your own skill set and knowledge

Leadership and humility

Networking

Learning to say 'no'

Learning to say 'yes'

Woman or a man?

Who's threatened?

Unconscious bias

Making a difference and giving back to others

#11　so are you going to go for it? 229

Reasons why you really shouldn't launch right now

Reasons why you should launch RIGHT NOW

#12　advice, guidance and inspiration from the best! 233

#13　a little about me 245

In the beginning

A rookie in business

Keeping in touch

Appendix : further reading

Books - a few ideas for your reading pile ...

*QR CODES

Throughout this book I have provided QR codes for you to easily link to websites, reports and books that I refer to. This saves you typing in the website address. If you are not familiar with QR codes please don't panic. They are just like bar codes. You can download a free app onto your phone or tablet that scans QR codes - they are all very straightforward to use. The biggest challenge is keeping your hand steady enough to scan the code whilst holding your phone in one hand, your coffee in the other and with this book balanced on your lap!

*CURRENCY CONVERSION

As you read you will see money issues come up on a frequent basis. I have put all money in pounds sterling. If you would like to convert money into a currency you are more familiar with here is a QR code for a currency converter:

Or otherwise why not use the quick conversion guide below (correct in August 2013):

UK POUNDS	£1	£10	£1000	£10000
US DOLLARS	$1.55	$15.51	$1550	$15509
SAUDI RIYALS	SR5.81	SR58.17	SR5817	SR58174
EUROS	€1.16	€11.62	€1161	€11615

CHAPTER ONE

ambition

a little thinking about ambition

Looking at what motivates and drives you, and what your fundamental ambitions in life are, is perhaps a good place to start this book.

But let me ask something perhaps a little contentious: is 'ambition' a dirty word if applied to a woman? Is it good to be ambitious? Is there a point at which, as a woman, you can be considered too ambitious? Are ambitious women admired and respected? And in asking, I am not asking about what people say publicly; I am asking about what people genuinely believe – because that is what will drive their behaviour towards you.

Call me old fashioned if you like, but I still see that society has every expectation that boys will be ambitious when at school and then, when they are men, that they will work to achieve their ambitions. Pretty single-mindedly at times! It's not always the same, though, when it comes to girls and women. Society is in a state of change and women's place in that is sometimes confusing. Some men and some women are absolutely cool with ambitious women. There are still plenty of both sexes, though, who are not, and plenty in between who sit on the fence!

Added to the complexity of differing views on ambition, there are of course the issues of society generally. Some societies talk very positively about girls and women developing their skills and leading businesses. Other societies frown upon both women's education and freedom to work. And don't be fooled into believing you can pinpoint which countries adopt which approach. If you want to read more on this, see the two examples I have set out later in this section.

Attitudes to female ambition are incredibly complex, so each of you will have to assess your own environment and work out where your support – as well as your challenges – will lie.

I like this quote: 'Women who strive to be equal to men lack ambition!'

two examples
one
In the UK there is endless talk in the press about the education and development of women in business. The message is out there that it is good to be ambitious and that society wants ambitious women. However, inevitably, a lot of women have babies and current medical advice for new mothers is to breastfeed for at least six months and if possible for twelve or more months. The World Health Organisation currently suggests breastfeeding for up to two years. The clear message given is that if you don't continue (or even start) to breastfeed you are not giving your child the best start in life. So how does that make ambitious women feel who really don't want to spend a year or more off work, but who equally don't want to be pegged as a 'bad or selfish mother'?

two
Many I have met in the US are proud to be part of a society leading the way in terms of the development and acceptance of women in business. I hear the same in Europe too. But did you know that in terms of women holding a director position on company boards this is the current state of affairs globally:

- Norway 40% (ranks 1st)
- South Africa 17%
- US 16.7%
- New Zealand 10%
- India 7% (ranks 28th in the world)
- Italy 4%

> Is this a ranking you would have expected and are these percentages acceptable? Perhaps some countries are where you thought they would be in ranking, whilst others are not? Last time I looked, Italy was in Europe, so what has happened there, for them to have such a disastrously low ranking? In fact it is not just a disastrously low ranking, but a shameful ranking. And why isn't the United States on a par with Norway? It should be and there should be no excuses why it is not. I had always thought the US led the way for the rest of the world in terms of being a progressive society, but perhaps in terms of women in leadership positions it has stalled. And New Zealand is incredibly low too at just 10%, particularly given that they had a female prime minister between 1999 and 2008.
>
> Western societies are often great at portraying themselves in the media as being progressive, but these figures show that all is not as it should be. We should be careful not to confuse freedom to be educated and freedom to work with genuine acceptance at senior levels in business and society.

I talked earlier about boys and men being encouraged to be ambitious. From my experience, girls are also often (but not always) encouraged to be ambitious when in education. In fact really serious ambition is often encouraged. But liberal views on the education and freedom of women can sometimes start to change when families and children come into the frame. I have also seen attitudes change when many years later, elderly relatives need care and there is absolutely no hesitation at times in expecting the daughter (or daughter in law) to give up her job or reduce her working hours, to take on the role.

I have seen the parents of successful women in their late twenties or thirties start to make noises about how it's time to stop playing careers and start to focus on family. I know that some partners and husbands begin to mutter about the state of the house or the lack of food in the fridge, or 'wouldn't it be better if you were able to spend more time at home while the children are so young?'

At work, you get married and go off on honeymoon a 'career women', but when you come back you find you are now viewed as a 'potential mother'.

And this is when bosses start to fudge issues around that promotion you were expecting and you might think the whole team you work with is waiting with baited breath for your tummy to start to swell!

And last but not least, stay at home mums at the school gate raise their eyebrows every time you are late for a pick up or forget it was a fancy dress day at school or bring a cake day or simply overlooked the fact that today was the last day of term. How was it that you thought there was at least another week to go? Have you ever done that? I have!

But who cares what society, parents, partners, husbands, friends and other mums think? Setting up and running a business is about your ambition and what you want for yourself. Not what others want for you or what others think you should be doing with your life.

So my first suggestion here is that ambition, and what others think of ambitious or working mothers, is just a minor irritation. Nothing more. Everyone has an opinion, so let them have theirs, but demonstrate your determination and independence of opinion by pursuing what you think is right for you and your family at this time in your life.

But perhaps you are one of those women who feel that spoken or unspoken opposition to your career plans is so overwhelming that you don't know if you even have the courage or fortitude to set up on your own. I know this is true of so many women in so many countries around the world. It's heartbreaking.

But to women in this position I suggest two things ...
First, think about whether you can start tiny and under the radar, perhaps just a small 'hobby' business at home that will upset or offend no-one. Then use this tiny business or hobby business to develop your skills and confidence and to build your knowledge. This way you might, over time, get other people adjusted to what you are doing, without it bruising egos or feeling threatening.

Second, don't go it alone. You are not alone. Know that many women across the world (even in the most 'civilised' societies) encounter serious obstacles to setting up in business, so tap into support networks and find like-minded women to talk to about this. You will find support if you have the courage to go out and look for it. Not all women want to support other woman in business, but there are plenty who do, so never feel you have to go it alone.

But now what I want you to do is decide just how ambitious you are right at this moment in time.

On a scale of 1-10, with 10 being 'couldn't be more ambitious' write your ambition number here:

I don't want you to write 10 just because you think that's what it ought to be. Write the number that accurately reflects how you currently feel. Now how do you feel about your number? Excited, scared, frustrated, anxious, determined? Take a few moments to think about how you feel about your ambition and what ambition means to you.

Next I would like you to think about how ambitious other women around you are. I'll explain my thinking behind this in just a minute. Give the women around you a number out of 10 too. But, again, don't give them a number that is idealistic, you have to be really honest here in order to get a proper picture.

Add in names and ambition scores for:

- ❖ Mother
- ❖ Female cousins
- ❖ Sisters
- ❖ Aunts
- ❖ Grandmother
- ❖ Sisters-in-law
- ❖ Neighbours

- ❖ Closest friends
- ❖ Mothers at the school gate
- ❖ Female teachers in your children's school
- ❖ Women in your book club
- ❖ Women in your Pilates or yoga class
- ❖ Women you currently work with
- ❖ Other important women around you

Now let's look at the men around you. Here I want to ask a slightly different question. Not how ambitious they are, but how supportive they are of women who are ambitious. In making your assessment think more about actions you have seen them take, rather than what they say about how supportive they are. Again, don't give any politically correct numbers. These numbers are for your eyes only. Challenge yourself on the scores you give. Make them really honest.

- ❖ Your husband/partner
- ❖ Father
- ❖ Brothers
- ❖ Grandfather
- ❖ Uncles
- ❖ Brothers-in-law
- ❖ Your friends' husbands and partners
- ❖ Men you currently work with
- ❖ Neighbours
- ❖ Friends of the family
- ❖ Men you meet socially

Now let me explain why I asked you to do this. From these scores for both men and women, you will start to get a sense of whether you are surrounded by a group of women and men who will really support you all the way and understand what you are striving for, or whether you are surrounded by people who will think you odd, different, scary, or someone to treat with caution. You will also get a sense of whether your support is more likely to come from home or outside your home, from the women or the men, from the older generations or the younger generations etc. You will also get an understanding of where you might encounter barriers.

You might think it odd me asking you to do this, but it's so important that you properly understand the motivations and support of the people around you, if you want to make your new business venture succeed. And be under no illusions about this, it is infinitely easier to succeed in business if you are surrounded by enthusiasts and supporters than if you have to battle your way through each day surrounded by doubters and pessimists.

In respect of your ambition scores for other women, it is absolutely not the case that people who are not ambitious themselves can not be (or will not be) supportive, but what they cannot perhaps do is provide the type of support that comes from understanding what you are doing, why you are doing it and what your day to day challenges are.

And in the list you now have of those who support your ambition, can I suggest you now go back and put a tick next to those who are likely to not only understand and support your ambition, but who can also provide you with actual business support or guidance.

This is important because if you go home at night after a month where you have made a loss of £3,000, £30,000 or £300,000, who do you really have to talk to who can understand what that means in business in terms of cash flow, annual profit/loss, business continuity etc.? Also, if you go home at night knowing that next day you are faced with having to speak in public to 100 people, who can truly support you with that, understand how you will be feeling and help you to perfect your speech? And finally, if you go home at night and want to share ideas about how to source a new IT system for work, who will you have to talk to about that? We all need support as we set up and grow our businesses and now is a great time for you to identify who around you can provide you with the different types of support you might need to be able to realise your ambitions.

> **NOTES:**
>
> write here the names of three people who are likely to most support you in your business venture:
>
> 1.
>
> 2.
>
> 3.

But don't despair if you have no-one to put into this list; what is important is that you recognise now that you need support and your task, of course, is to stop looking down-hearted, and instead start building from scratch a support network. As with so many obstacles in business, first identify the difficulty, then think positively about how to overcome it.

We will talk more about networking in business in a later chapter if this is of interest to you.

a quick story for you about ambition ...

I have a friend who is brilliant at making glass jewellery. It's her hobby. I spent about three years gently encouraging her to set up a business and sell her work commercially. Her children were growing up and she wanted to get back into work. When she did eventually set up her business, I have to acknowledge, the time was right for her. Earlier, when I first started encouraging her, it just wouldn't have been the right time for her and where her ambitions were at.

Just a year or so after setting up her business, my friend was in a top London department store browsing. A sales lady approached and said she had spotted her jewellery the minute she walked in. The sales lady then asked her whether she had made the jewellery herself and also whether she sold her jewellery commercially.

The store was currently looking for a new collection of jewellery along the lines of what my friend was wearing and would she be interested in meeting the buyer who happened to be in the store today? My friend said 'yes'. Who wouldn't! But by the time the sales lady had reappeared with the store's buyer, my friend had gone. Disappeared! But why?

Selling your designs to a top London store just a year after setting up in business might have sounded like an opportunity of a lifetime to many, but what you have to know and accept in setting up a business is that you can only go at the pace your self-confidence allows you to go. And you really don't have to worry about what other people think you should do.

No regrets. No self-recriminations. That's just the way it is. Be comfortable with who you are and where you are in business today and know that you really don't have to run before you feel able to walk ... unless you really want to!

what motivates you?

Over the years I have delivered lots of training sessions on motivation. I find it a fascinating topic as so many of us assume that everyone around us is motivated by the same things we are. There also seems to be a seldom-questioned belief that everyone who sets up and runs their own business is motivated by money (with the exception, of course, of those who set up charities and social enterprises).

And why would anyone question the statement that money is the primary motivator for all that we do? The media expects all business people to be motivated by money (and be endlessly greedy for it), society expects it, our families expect it, our educators expect it. What is there in the literature we read and the education we receive that ever suggests that the primary reason to set up in business is not money?

But what if by any small chance you do set up in business, but are not motivated by making piles of money? Perhaps your motivator is job satisfaction or proving to yourself that you can do it? But if you are not driven by a need to make as much money as is humanly possible, what might the repercussions be?

- ❖ Lack of respect from other business owners?
- ❖ Successful men (and women) saying that you don't have what it takes to succeed in business?
- ❖ Imbalanced relationships with your clients and suppliers who don't understand that always getting the best price or the best deal is not your priority?
- ❖ Lack of respect in society when you do not make those millions?
- ❖ A reduction in your own drive as it is not clear exactly what you are driving for?
- ❖ People struggling to understand what you are about and therefore suggesting that you are not successful?
- ❖ Staff questioning whether you know what you are doing, which might jeopardise their loyalty to you and your business?

I am sure that many of you reading this book will be motivated by money and that is fine, but I know without a doubt that many of you will not. But exactly how do you explain yourself when you say that you are setting up in business but that the sole purpose of your business is not to make a huge profit? Just saying this could well be enough to make your bank manager go pale in the face and stare at you as though you come from outer space!

> Just as an aside, even those not motivated by money will of course want to earn some money in order to pay for the roof over their heads, food for the table and other essentials in life. But where they are different, is that they are not motivated to earn more money than the next person, or become viewed as someone who is wealthy. If you want to read a bit more about motivation then why not take a look at some research on this subject such as Maslow's hierarchy of needs or some of the work on motivation by Herzberg.

Recently, Aspire did some great research into women leaders

 *scan me

This is what they found about women's career priorities in 2013:

1. Satisfaction with my team
2. Challenging work
3. Satisfaction with my manager
4. Satisfaction with company culture
5. Recognition
6. Making a difference to others

7. Belief in company direction
8. Money
9. Upward progression
10. Job security

how would you rank these 10 different criteria in respect of what motivates you?

For me, the rankings on this list come as no surprise at all. Women seek satisfaction at work, recognition for what they do, the opportunity to make a difference and the opportunity to be challenged and stretched. Discussing with male business owners the exact point at which they aim to be a million- or billionaire doesn't even make the list for most women.

I would be curious, though, to know how many women pretend that money is their sole motivator in order to gain acceptance in the male business community, or otherwise to explain to their families their crazy hours and incredible dedication to business.

This list does of course create a challenge for male/female business partnerships when the motivations of the two parties can be so different. Personally, I would be curious to know how many men listen to a woman when she says her primary motivation in business is not money, but who fail to really hear or accept what she is saying. This inevitably causes friction and difficulty down the line.

> 'Listening' to the words but not 'hearing' the message is the cause of so many miscommunications and misunderstandings in business. Are you ever guilty of this?

I suspect also that we uncover a fundamental issue with business financing across the globe if we start to talk about many female business owners not being solely driven by profits. Banks and investors value a return on investment. In fact they most value those clients who can consistently demonstrate an ability to maximise the return on investment.

Banks and investors are not interested in the slightest in charitable donations, how many you employ, from what parts of the community they come, and whether you source your products locally or ethically.

Women, though, appear to value making enough money to put back into society. They value making a difference to their own lives and to the lives of others. But how is this compatible with the way society views success in business? Perhaps this is why some suggest that women 'play' at business rather than take it seriously.

So do women need to change what motivates them or do men at the top of our men's business world need to re-think how they evaluate and judge success? Of course, the most powerful solution would be to have a combined approach in the top tier of each business, with each gender bringing its own strengths to the table.

self-employed or entrepreneur ?

Putting ambition and motivation aside for now, I thought I would just clear up a bit of thinking around owning a business and becoming a female entrepreneur.

In a nutshell, it is estimated that around 95-99% of business owners view themselves as self-employed. Fewer than 5% view themselves as an entrepreneur. Many differentiate between the two by saying that owning a business is just like doing a job for someone else – only this time you are the boss, so they are your decisions, your clients, your sales, your money etc.

Entrepreneurship, on the other hand, is often viewed as something more than self-employment. Entrepreneurs don't just run the business; they are constantly looking for new ideas and new ways to make money, they employ others, they build businesses and they create money for both themselves and others.

Many women set up in business with absolutely no intention of ever employing anyone else, expanding out of their home or taking the world by storm. They set up perhaps to keep themselves busy, to earn money, to challenge themselves, to show their friends and family that they really can do it. Not all women, of course, take this approach, but many do.

So when does someone who is self-employed become an entrepreneur? For me it doesn't matter where you draw the line or what you call yourself and the reality of course is that little in business pans out the way you expect it to so ... self-employed today, international entrepreneur tomorrow!

> If you haven't read any books by Margaret Mead, you might take a look at some of her work. This is one of her quotes that I like:
>
> 'Never doubt that a small group of thoughtful, committed citizens can change the world; indeed, it's the only thing that ever has.'

CHAPTER TWO

thinking things through

what do you want?

> The most entrepreneurial age group for females is 35–44 years.

It's interesting that not many people take the time when setting up in business to really think through what they want. What they want is sort of in their consciousness, but not necessarily thought through and properly considered. Are you drifting into business too or do you already have spreadsheets and business plans wallpapering your sitting room?

> **A few interesting facts and figures for you before we begin ...**
> - 48% of female entrepreneurs own businesses in the service sector, compared with 36% of male entrepreneurs.
> - Female entrepreneurs are more likely than male entrepreneurs:
>   - to sell a product or service unfamiliar to the market
>   - to have fewer competitors
>   - to be using the latest technology in their products or services

> o to be offering a product or service to the market that has been developed in the last year.
>
> ❖ Women are nearly five times more likely to mention family reasons for becoming self-employed than men.
> ❖ Men are twice as likely as women to say that one of the reasons they became self-employed was to 'make more money'.

Now here are a few of my ideas to get your brain cells going about what you really want from your business … (I suggest you make some notes as you read.)

legacy/thought leadership

Do you want to run a business so you can leave your mark on the world?

Do you want it to lead the way in the market place, or are you content to follow the lead set by other businesses?

travel

Do you want to travel? If so, where to, what sort of travel, how often, how far?

money

Do you want to earn pin money, a bit more than pin money, similar to what you are earning now, a lot more than you are earning now, or do you want to make serious money?

If you could give a percentage importance to you of job satisfaction versus financial return, where would the balance be? 70% job satisfaction and 30% financial return? Or the other way around?

If you sell your time by the hour, the amount you make in a year will be limited by the number of hours you have. If you want to make more money than that do you accept that you will need to employ staff?

If you sell a high-expertise service which has a higher profit margin, you may well make good money when the business is just you, but you might find it expensive to expand, as staffing and recruitment costs could be very high. In contrast, you might find it much easier and cheaper to develop and build a business based around low expertise or low skill. What sort of business do you want to build?

If you make (or purchase) goods to sell, your earnings will not be limited in the same way as if you are just selling hours, so volume of sales on goods could be the route to achieving a better profit margin, provided you have the capital to buy the goods to sell. Is this your preferred option?

What profit margin are you aiming to have and is this realistic for the industry sector you are in? (More on profit margins later in this chapter.)

family/hours

Do you want to (can you if necessary) work weekends and/or nights?
Do you want to work from home?

Do you want flexible hours that enable you to work around family commitments?

Could you adjust your working hours to cover different time zones around the world, or would that result in you having no work/life balance?

structure/set-up

Do you want to work for yourself, offering your existing skill set to those who will value you and pay you for your services?

Do you want to set up and grow a small business?

Do you want to set up and build a large business? Or perhaps you want to start small and then get seriously ambitious in a few years time when the time is right?

Do you want to set up a hobby business? Something that enables you to earn some money from your hobby or a business that you can treat like a hobby? A business that will give you fun, a sense of satisfaction, and will earn you money, but is never likely to make you rich and famous?

Will your business be a charity or social enterprise? Will your profit-making business aim to give a percentage of profit to charity or the community every year?

Do you want to continue to use your existing skills as your business grows, or do you see a time when you will stop doing what you were originally trained to do because now your daily job is to run or grow the business?

Do you want to go it alone or do you want to find a business partner? Perhaps you want to seek external financing and are happy to sacrifice some control of the business for that?

the future

Do you want to build a business to sell in five years, or a business for your children to inherit? Perhaps you want to build a business that can provide employment for your partner in a few years' time. Or perhaps it's about providing employment in the local community?

Do you want to run an international business?

personal factors

Do you want to run the business anonymously (i.e. from an office or computer) or do you want to be more front-facing and have a public profile?

Do you want your business to reflect your personal values in life?

Do you want to run a business to prove someone wrong about you?

Do you want to run a business to prove to yourself you can do it?

Do you want the sense of power that comes from running a business, or is it more important that you get the sense of satisfaction that comes from running a business?

> Lots of questions, I know, but what I have set out above is by no means an exhaustive list. It is merely intended to give you a guide and help you focus your thoughts. But from what you have read so far, if I asked you to sum up in just ten words what you want from the business you are setting up (or already running), what would you say?

a little bit about profit margins

Another consideration in deciding what kind of business to go for is what profit margin you want. I mentioned this in the previous section. If you are financially trained or familiar with company financials, I suggest you skip right on to the next section.

In the early days of a business, some confuse turnover with profit. The two are very different things, though. In very simple terms, the profit margin is what you are left with when you deduct your costs from your sales! Many female entrepreneurs set up in business without giving any thought whatsoever to their profit margin. In fact I am sure that many male entrepreneurs do too! I confess to having done this in the very early days of setting up; I just assumed that if I worked hard enough the money would sort itself!

it's easy to make a loss!

Many small business owners I know forget to factor in their own time or expenses when calculating profit margins. In hindsight they discover that the profitable business they thought they were running, is in fact making a loss. Let me give you an example:

If you buy ten boxes of chocolates for a total of £20 and sell them on for £40, to properly calculate the profit margin, as well as the cost of the chocolates, you probably need to factor in the time taken for both buying and selling your goods (let's assume two hours in total and you value your time at £10/hour) and also the £5 in petrol it cost you to collect your goods and take them to the place of sale. Your profit calculation is therefore as follows:

+ £40 sales (i.e. turnover)
- £5 (petrol)
- £20 (chocolates)
- £20 (time)
= Loss of £5

turning a loss into a profit

But if, as a result of doing your business planning, you know in advance that just buying ten boxes at £2 each will result in a loss, then instead you buy sixty boxes at £1.50 each (given that now you are buying in sufficient quantity to be able to negotiate).
And whilst it will take an extra hour to sell this quantity, your end result will look like this:

+ £240 sales (your turnover)
- £5 (petrol)
- £90 (chocolates)
- £30 (time)
= Profit of £115

I know someone who operates a multi-million pound business that he inherited from his father. It has several hundred staff and operates on a net profit margin of around 1%. That means if he turns over £5 million his profit is typically going to be only £50K each year or, if it was a start-up business turning over £500,000, his profit would be only £10,000 a year. That's a lot of effort and hassle for a small return. It also means that his business is at constant risk, as it would take only one or two legal claims or bad debts in a year for his whole profit to be wiped out. If he were setting up from scratch, knowing that this was his likely profit margin for the next twenty years, do you think he would have bothered to even open the doors on the first day for business?

I also know many who run their business on a profit margin of 10%. This is where it starts to feel more comfortable. Then quite a few I know have a 20% profit margin. Thinking about some I know who sell products rather than services, there are several who have a 35-40% profit margin and I even know a designer who aims for a 200% profit margin on her work. So what profit margin are you anticipating in your business, and is it appropriate given the industry sector you are in?

If you have no idea about profit margins in your industry sector then I really would recommend you do some research.

But before you go off and do that, how about putting an initial profit margin figure here. You can always change it later.

> **NOTES:**
>
> **what is the minimum profit margin you will be looking for?**

But what if you have already set up in a business that has a very low profit margin? Is it too late to aim higher?

It's hard if you have set up a business that has great customers and a good reputation, but that has a tiny profit margin, to now decide to close it down in order to set up something different with a bigger profit margin. I understand this because at the end of the day you want to feel like you will eventually get the right financial return given your time and money investment. Plus this endeavour has probably been like your baby.

But: do you want your decision-making in business to be driven by your emotions? By all means take into consideration your emotions around your business, but if you choose to continue to run a business with little or no profit margins, then don't turn around in ten years time with regrets about having earned so little despite so much hard graft.

If your profit margin is a problem, take action now to either move into a new business, or morph your existing business into a business that is offering services or products with a good profit margin so it gives you a sensible return for your effort and financial investment.

When I set up my first business, my only thought was how I could sell the service I was currently delivering within a corporate environment to small and medium sized enterprises (SMEs) who would appreciate me more than my last employer had. I didn't think bigger than that. I didn't think about how I would grow, or what my profit margin would be or whether there was a different sort of business I could run. In reality, of course, I played it safe and stuck to what I knew best and knew would be of value to others.

No harm in playing it safe though. But I would encourage you to think through whether playing it safe at the beginning might limit your ability to grow or turn a profit in the future.

> Did you know ... that female entrepreneurs typically put back 70-80% of the money they earn into the local community? In contrast, male entrepreneurs put back around 30-40%.
>
> Have you given any thought as to whether you might want to put something back into your local (or the wider) community? What sort of project would give you immense satisfaction?

NOTES

Time to think about you ... having read this far, it might be a good time for you to make some more notes about what you want from a business. Fill in as much as you feel ready to. You can always come back and change it later!

Money (turnover, profit margin)

Travel

Hours

Sector

Product or service

Staff

Developing your own skills

A business to build to sell or build to pass on

Other

a business for your retirement

I haven't covered this topic in the section on 'what do you want', but feel that setting up a business after retirement merits a short section all of its own.

I come across a lot of people who spend years waiting to be paid off by their employer or waiting to retire so that they can then set up a business.

It's interesting, though, that whilst many dream for years of setting up a business, most have no clear idea of what kind of business they want – just that they want to set up a business. Often they have a clear understanding of the type of environment they want to work in, or the values their fledgling business will have, or what it will give back to the community, but not exactly what the nature of the business will be.

I am no psychologist but how can it be that you dream about a business venture for five or even ten years but still have no concept of what service you will provide or what products you will sell? Is it because you just enjoy dreaming but don't actually want to bring anything to fruition, or is it because you feel achieving it is just so distant, you delay any serious planning?

I hope that some of the content of this book will help some of you make it feel less distant and unachievable. There are, though, a few things I will include here just for you:

- ❖ Pin down the idea for your business – be disciplined enough to make some decisions about what it is you want to do.
- ❖ Set a limit – a really clear limit – on how much you will invest in this venture across the first three years. And please, please don't go pouring half your retirement fund into it.
- ❖ Be considerate of your energy levels (it's hard, I know, but you need to accept that 99% of you will not have the energy levels of a thirty-year-old, so be realistic).
- ❖ Talk to others who have set up a business following retirement. Write down your values for how you wish to do business.

- Write down what, in no more than five years' time, you want to have achieved.
- Be clear as to whether this is an ongoing venture that you will continue for as long as you are able-bodied or whether you just intend to have a delayed retirement date.
- Check to see where your partner/husband is with your plans, because if he wants to play golf, or sit down with his feet up to watch sports on TV or travel the world, but you want to double your working hours, you might have problems!

a business with young children

As with setting up a business post-retirement, I wanted to just touch on a few specifics relating to setting up a business to enable you to work whilst you have a young family to look after.

There is so little truly flexible employment available that setting up a business around childcare commitments is common. It provides a way for the mother to continue working, for her to be able to contribute to the finances of the household, whilst still managing the house and bringing up the children. It's a win/win situation provided you set up the right business and make it work for you.

When I set up in business, this is effectively what I was doing. I worked part time from home. My clients thought I worked full time, but in reality I spent the day juggling jobs.

In hindsight this is what worked really well when it was just me working from home in those early days and this is what didn't work so well:

the good stuff:

- ❖ I saw lots of my children as they were growing up.
- ❖ I never had to apologise for taking time out to attend a sports day or go to a music concert at the school.
- ❖ I never went mad due to not being able to use my brains or stretch myself.
- ❖ My children grew up in a household with high work ethic.
- ❖ I didn't have to do so much housework (which I hate!) as I could employ someone to help.
- ❖ I could start late in the morning after doing the various school runs and no-one could complain. Equally my working day could finish when I wanted it to and again there was no one around to complain about me not pulling my weight!

the not so good stuff:

- ❖ I neglected my own health and welfare as I was so busy juggling household, children and business with no let-up for a break in the evenings or at weekends.
- ❖ It got really stressful dealing with phone calls if there were children being noisy in the background. No clients like to think of you not totally focused on them!
- ❖ It was very easy to work late at night or into the night if I needed to, but the downside of that was that it blurred the boundaries of downtime.
- ❖ For me it felt like a halfway house in terms of career, which in turn affected my view of myself as a business owner and meant that I undervalued my services and my skills.

It wasn't so much a problem for me, but a few women I know went into business to build their confidence and earn a little money, but ended up providing a lousy service due to being continually drawn away from work into family matters. A common feature was that they failed to deliver on time, they provided a poor quality service, they neglected the important stuff such as the financial accounts, and they ended up pulled in so many different directions that they were continually stressed.

My observations from this are that if your family considers you not only the prime carer of your children, but also the person to come to in a crisis for all your nieces, nephews, elderly aunts, uncles, sisters, brothers and parents etc. as well, if you never learn to say 'no' or teach your family where the boundaries lie between personal time and work time, setting up a business might at times seem more of a punishment than a pleasure.

can you have it all?

Throughout the past twenty years I have listened to the debate about whether women can have it all: a serious career and a family.

The reality is that you can have it all. But the greater reality is that having it all has now resulted in a massive problem of women burning out in their forties. This isn't good for them, for their families, or for the economy that needs to keep these skilled women in work.

Women so often feel they have to work harder to prove themselves at work, and if you combine this with the gruelling demands of looking after and raising young children, it's not so surprising that one day, your energy just runs out. And it takes a long time to recover from exhaustion like that.

So yes you can have it all, but probably for a limited period only. My advice to all of you wanting to combine running a business with raising children is to remember that your career and working life is more like a marathon than a sprint. Conserve your energy so you can still walk upright when you get to age sixty!

a business because no-one else will give you a job!

If anyone asks me about employment, I usually smile and say I am proud to be totally unemployable! The reality of course is that if I needed to, I am sure I could slot right back into one of the corporate beasts that leave you wondering what on earth you have achieved each year and whether anyone actually knows you exist. But for the most part I am proud to now be so multi-skilled, so independent, so determined, that most businesses would not know what to do with me.

But unlike people like me who have become 'unemployable' as a result of running our own businesses, there are many who choose to set up in business because they already view themselves as unemployable.

Over the years I have done some mentoring and coaching with people who are homeless but who want to get back to a state of financial independence. It is a pretty rare employer who would even bother to look at the CV of someone who is currently homeless, so the route to financial independence for many of our homeless is through setting up their own business.

I once had a conversation with a woman who was just setting up her business and she told me that when seeking a start-up loan from a local charity she had decided that her first purchase was going to be a kettle. If women think they have it tough setting up a business, then homeless women have barriers the rest of us cannot even being to imagine. However, as I have said before, there is support out there if you really want it. It might take a bit of looking for, you might have to accept a few knock-backs, but there are enough people out there who will support you if you are homeless and want to set up in business and achieving financial independence is worth the effort and knock-backs as it will provide you with so many more choices in life.

A few years ago, I heard that on the streets of London around 18% of homeless people were university-educated. No kettle, but they have a degree!

From working with people who are homeless, here are a few of my tips if you want to set up in business:

- If you find a mentor or coach, you have to hold on to them. Missing meetings because you forgot what day it is, cancelling because you think a session can be held tomorrow instead of today is just not workable, so you need to organise yourself and start thinking of yourself as a business person even if you haven't quite got there yet.

- Communicate what your issues are, because those of us who have not been homeless would never know that your priority is a kettle rather than a laptop, or that you might have a laptop, but what on earth can you do to protect that when everything you take each night into a homeless hostel gets stolen overnight. But if you don't help us to understand the real day-to-day challenges, we will be busy focusing on the business plan instead of what really matters at this early stage.

- Don't be so determined to help other homeless people get off the streets that you employ too many people in your social enterprise, run out of cash and go bust. To help others, you have to put your business on a profitable footing first.

- Don't get to rely on charity such as free start-up loans, free mentoring, free coaching. You need to put a plan in place to use these to get going but then quickly wean yourself off what is available to you free of charge, otherwise you will never get your attitude right about the value of money and the real costs of running a business.

- From the very beginning you need to act 'as if' – that is, you need to think (and have the self-belief) that you are a business person, that you are already running a successful business, that you are making money, that you have a plan and are achieving it. This means that you need to look the part – wash up and brush up as best you can, have clothes kept for you somewhere safe and dry that support rather than hinder your business endeavours; your shoulders need to be back, your head held high and if you struggle to make eye contact, then practise this day in and day out until you do feel you can look people in the eye.

- ❖ Build a network of contacts who can guide and support you and make it your responsibility to keep in regular touch with them to avoid them drifting away or forgetting who you are. And don't just think about business contacts, find contacts who can store dry clothes for your business meetings, contacts who can lock up your laptop at night, contacts who are great listeners for the times you just need to offload, contacts who can help you create a focus in business etc. All kinds of contacts. Many start with virtually no contacts at all, so this is probably something you will need to work hard at from the very moment you decide to go into business.

And for others of you who also think you are unemployable – those just out of prison, those who have left the sex trade, those who have escaped after being trafficked into the country, those whose lives have collapsed due to alcoholism, drug addiction, mental illness, family trauma, horrific life-changing experiences – setting up and running your own business could well be a real lifesaver for you as well as bringing financial independence. Many of the tips I have given above will also apply to you. But if you just want to focus on two, then make them the last two! You need to act 'as if' and you need a good network. I suggest you make those your starting point.

A big issue, of course, for many who find themselves 'unemployable' is self-belief that they can do this and can achieve financial independence and security. But you can do it. It is possible to turn your life and fortunes around. Many have done it already. Here are a few things that might help:

- ❖ Surround yourself with people who will encourage you and keep you on track.
- ❖ Every day when you wake up, focus on where you are going and what you are going to achieve.
- ❖ Don't allow yourself even a few moments of doubt; focus on being positive.
- ❖ Read about others who have achieved and be inspired by their stories.

> two favourite sayings of mine:
>
> 'where there's a will, there's a way'
> 'never give up! try and try and try again!'

what are you going to sell?

So many women over the years have talked to me about their dreams to set up in business, but admit that they still don't know what they will sell. I have found this particularly in Saudi Arabia but I'm sure it occurs in every country. This section is for those of you who have a dream to be in business, but who need support with thinking through your business ideas.

It's really hard for me to give you ideas about what to sell as so much will depend on what you know, what you like, what you think you can do, and what you want to do etc. But let me put forward just a few ideas and pointers.

product or service?

A starting point might be to think about whether you want to sell

- a product (e.g. beauty products, insurance policies);
- a service (designing websites, translation company);
- both product and service (restaurant, e learning courses).

If you have a product to sell your outlet typically will be:

- a shop
- an office
- market or other temporary stalls or fairs
- through a distribution network
- online
- a combination of any or all of the above!

And either you will be looking to buy in your product to sell, or manufacture your own product; or design the product, but then outsource the manufacturing of it.

If you sell a service you might consider whether you will be delivering via phone, face to face, across the internet or a combination of all of these.

copying others' business ideas

Should you sell products or services your friends and/or relatives already sell? Or perhaps there has been a business you admire that you have been watching for a while that is owned by someone you don't even know?

Sometimes I find that people decide to set up a business virtually identical to a business already set up and trading – often by one of their relatives or friends. I am sure there is a sense of 'safe' in this. You know there is a market; you know the price points etc., so you have a clear route forward.

However, you will have to decide some critical issues such as if the market is saturated already and whether you will be able to differentiate yourself from others selling the same thing.

In contrast, should you set up a business that no one else you know is running, you will need to understand who will buy from you, at what price and in what sort of quantities. You might therefore need to do some market research during your planning stage. You might also take the exciting entrepreneurial view that the marketplace is yours for the taking and that it could lead to much more of an adventure than setting up a business in a crowded market place.

B2B or B2C?

Another essential decision is do you want to run a business that sells to other businesses or do you want to sell to consumers?

If you want to sell B2B (business-to-business) are you going to sell to small businesses, medium sized businesses or large corporates? Perhaps you want to sell to charities or the public sector? Where are your customers and how will they want to buy from you?

If you want to sell B2C (business-to-consumer) do you want to sell small ticket items (e.g. corporate gifts, chocolates, beauty treatments) or large ticket items (e.g. vehicles, property, top end jewellery)? What age group will be your target market and what sector of society? Where are your customers and how will they want to buy from you?

brainstorming your business idea

If you have already spent a year or more thinking about setting up a business but still don't know what you are going to sell, then perhaps now is the time to take some real time out to think about what product or service you can/will sell.

Here are a few ideas for how you might go about brainstorming your business idea:

Brainstorming often works best when three or more people are involved. Consider bringing in some friends or advisors to help you brainstorm.

Stop/start – one brainstorming technique is to spend one minute with everyone contributing ideas. You then all take a further minute when everyone is silent. This provides an opportunity for individuals to reflect on ideas put forward so far and also to come up with more ideas on their own. You then start the process again; one minute group thinking and one minute reflecting.

Day one/two/three – another technique is to meet to brainstorm all the ideas for twenty to thirty minutes one day. Then let the ideas mull over individually until you meet again on day two for another round of twenty to thirty minutes' brainstorming, which can either seek to come up with entirely new ideas, or otherwise build on the ideas you came up with the day before. You then have a further opportunity to reflect before meeting for a final round.

Make it visual – write all the ideas up on a board so people can see them and reflect. If you don't write ideas down as you come up with them, you might forget some great ideas and only remember the last ones to have been put on the table.

Touch – some people find it easier to think when they are touching things. You might want to wander around a shop or market place looking at what is being sold, touching what is being sold, thinking about what you would like to buy in that place and thinking about what it is they do not yet sell. Thinking on the move is brilliant for some people. Others, though, like really quiet reflective time – so decide what works for you and then create that environment.

Sounding boards – don't run your great business idea past your best friend or mother. They will always say what a great idea it is. If you are serious about business, find some people who won't always flatter your ego and praise what you do. You need some critical thinkers around you for them to be a really useful sounding board. As a suggestion, why not think about who is likely to dismiss your idea and approach them first!

> Getting into the mood for creative thinking can sometimes be the challenge. I believe that all of us have the ability to be creative; therefore it is often a case of finding a way to bring out our own creativity. One exercise I have used many times is to organise three or four people around a table. Get comfortable and then between you, take no more than ten minutes to brainstorm five potential (but unexpected) uses of each of the following: a paperclip; a doughnut; a tub of butter; a scarf; a pencil. Once you have five uses for each of these you then take a few minutes to discuss the ideas you came up with, and then start again. This time you need to build on some of the uses put forward first time. I often find that this second round encourages greater creativity, much more humour and risk-taking as ideas are put forward. As a final round you then take ten minutes to discuss and choose between you one of the ideas put forward for each item in rounds one or two that you think could provide the greatest commercial opportunity: i.e. this time you start to think about taking a creative idea to market. It's a fun exercise so why not give it a go!

assessing if your business idea will fly

> Got a business idea?
>
> Before you get carried away, this is what I was once told to ask:
>
> 'Would I buy what I am selling, from me?'
>
> You have to be honest with yourself. Really honest with yourself! If the answer is no, then you need to rethink and then adapt your idea until such point as you are really clear that what you are selling, you would yourself buy from your business.
>
> If you want to say 'yes', but deep down know that the answer is 'no', then perhaps its time to take some time out to come up with another business idea.

Here are a few suggestions from me for how you might test whether your idea is a good one or not:

- Can you produce your amazing gadget for less than the price at which you wish to sell it at? If you can't, then bin the whole idea.
- Is there enough market for what you want to sell? Realistically, what percentage of the population or how many businesses will be in your marketplace? Are there enough of them for you ever to sell enough of your product/service to make a profit?
- If this is a new concept, will it require you to educate people about what your product can do for them before you can even begin to sell it? If so, what budget do you have for educating the world and do you have the time and energy to do that educating before you even begin to sell?
- What will differentiate your product or service from the business next door, and is it enough of a differentiator for you to steal some of their market share? If there is virtually no differentiator, you may be in trouble.

- How much will it cost you to get the accreditations, quality marks, safety certificates etc. that you need to bring this to market, and can you afford all of that?
- How much capital and how much time will it take to realistically bring this to market? Do you have enough of both or could it bankrupt you before you are ever ready to sell?
- If you took this idea to an investor would they laugh at you, smile indulgently at you or would they want to start talking figures?
- Producing one widget is often easy enough, but what will it take to produce enough of them for you to have a business? Do you have the premises, staff, machines and capital it will require? And if you decide you need to get on a plane to China to find a manufacturer, does that thought fill you with excitement or dread?
- Could you see yourself selling this product or service for the next ten or twenty years?
- Is this really what you want to be selling? Are you passionate enough about it? Does this business idea excite you?
- Who will buy this and what price would they expect? Does your target market have the sort of money required to buy your product or service?
- Do you know enough about the market you want to sell into to really understand what they will be looking for, what price they will expect to pay and what might put them off buying from you?
- Does your product look home- or handmade and if so, will that prevent you from selling it?
- Has anyone tried to sell something similar and failed in their business venture?

and finally ...

- What question are you desperately hoping I will not ask, as you know it could well blow your idea out of the water?

If you have thought it through, here is an opportunity to commit your idea to paper:

What idea do you have for a business?

What are your solid reasons, facts, figures and other relevant information for believing this idea will fly? (no woolly or fluffy answers allowed!)

NOTES

exit strategies to decide before you get going

It might seem odd to think about your exit strategy before you have even set up or really got going, but I would encourage you not to neglect this bit of thinking.

Many women I know take the view that they will set up, see how it goes, build it up if its looking successful, just keep it ticking along if it's not so successful, run it until they get bored or run out of steam and then decide what to do next.

As strategies go, this isn't the greatest (note the British understated humour there!).

> a little story about understanding your 'end point'.
>
> This is about a project rather than a business, but the point is the same. For many years I sat on the fundraising committee of my children's village school. Once a year we aimed to raise as much as we could on one day by holding a village fayre with stalls and entertainment. Not wishing to muscle in on those who were taking the lead, I often tried to encourage some thinking about what we were aiming to make financially before we planned the stalls and events. In one particular year I suggested we speak to the fundraising teams of two other villages that were raising huge sums consistently year on year with a view to finding out what they were doing so well and that we could learn from. But no-one wanted to listen and for some reason no-one wanted to even discuss setting targets. There was more a sense of 'we'll just do what seems like a good idea and hope that makes us a good profit'.

For me, though, it was so frustrating. They spent so much time organising such a huge event but no-one really thought about the end point – the point at which we counted up the money and decided whether all our efforts had been worth it. Ultimately, of course, this meant that in some years the instincts and approach of the person leading it were spot-on and we made good money, but in the majority of years there was an endless succession of missed opportunities. But whoever was running it and whatever money we made, we were never really able to congratulate ourselves at having hit a target – you would have to have a target to be able to do that!

> 'If you don't know where you are headed,
> how will you know when you get there?'

But returning to exit strategies, here are a few options:

- Sell within a set timescale (in 5 years, 10 years, at retirement etc.).
- Run the business until you retire then hand it over to a general manager (or equivalent) so you still own it and it funds your retirement.
- Run the business until you have a family member ready and waiting in the wings to take control of the reins.
- Run the business but take time too to develop your management team, building within them an expectation that when you are ready to retire they will buy you out.
- Run the business, take money from it, then when you want out, simply close it down – no sale. (This might be sensible for those who sell their own time so would have no real business to sell in five years' time.)

If you set up with a view to selling, the timescale is of course important. Let me explain. If you set up with a view to selling it in five years' time then you will probably structure it very differently than if you plan to sell it in twenty years' time when you retire.

To sell a business, typically investors will look at your cost base and your profits from at least the past three years. They will of course look at a lot more besides, but these two are important as if you set up with a view to selling in five years' time, in reality you have no time to build it up and then look to trim back overheads or rack up the profit when you are ready to sell. You need to be doing that from day one and be doing that day in, day out with no distractions.

However if you set up with a view to selling in twenty years' time you have around fifteen years to grow your business as you want to grow it, without feeling you need to permanently keep costs as low as possible, maximise profit at every turn and not worry about whether your clients will be with you in six years' time. You can then begin to restructure it with a view to making it attractive for sale around four to five years before actually selling.

For my part, I had an exit strategy in mind almost from the beginning. I set up the business with the intention of growing it so I could sell it at the end of my career and it would fund my retirement. My husband at the time had a good job and his own good pension, and we agreed that whilst I could run a business, there was no need for me to take money out of the business in the short term (i.e. pay myself market rates and dividends). We agreed that the best strategy was for me to keep money in the business and reinvest that money for growth. This would ensure that at the point of sale when I reached retirement age, we would have maximised growth.

There were, though, a few flaws in the plan.

- ❖ At the point at which I got divorced, the cost base of the business was such that I could not suddenly start to draw a market rate salary. What should have brought me financial independence, thirteen years into running a business had not actually brought me any independence at all.

- If you, as the business owner, are not taking a salary or dividends, what is there to really motivate you day on day? What is going to make you hungry for sales and growth?

- Setting up a business which will give you a payday thirty years hence is nonsensical. How can anyone measure their own value and gain a sense of achievement if the payday – bonus time – is so far away? As a business owner you have to have goals that are more tangible, otherwise you lose focus and drive.

- But the most crucial flaw in the plan was what it did to my head! Within the family we thought of my business as a hobby. My husband said it was my hobby. I told myself it was my hobby. But when you tell yourself your business is just your hobby because you don't actually need the money it can generate, it is never going to be structured and grown in a way that will result in a great retirement pot. I learnt that the hard way.

So your exit strategy is crucial as it gives you:

- a sense of purpose
- the right mental attitude
- a framework for how your business should be structured and grown
- a way for you to measure your achievements and successes.

One other thing I learnt about exit strategies along the way is that you really ought to take good advice about how to structure your business with a view to exiting. The reality is that most investors and purchasers of businesses are men. Men might value in your business something different to what you yourself value. You need to know what that is if you are to maximise your opportunities to sell.

As an example, if you have a long-term vision for the brand you have been carefully building, don't be disheartened if the investor you are talking to cares nothing about your brand and is only interested in whether current sales projections will give him the right return on investment within twenty-four months. I find that women take a much longer term view of business and often have a more holistic view of it – but don't expect these views to be reciprocated by your investor or purchaser.

It is also a sad fact that my experience over the years has been that many men like to buy from men – particularly when it comes to large purchases such as cars, houses and businesses – and probably yachts too, although I have no experience of that! I imagine it gives them a comfort factor and a sense that everyone is speaking the same language. Many men still believe that women in the business world come from a different universe and speak some unintelligible language! If you want to make a point, by all means head up your own negotiations. But the whole process can at times be simpler and quicker if you appoint a man to act for you. For my part there are times when I have decided I am going to go into battle – yet again – and gear myself up to be really assertive and 'manly' in my communication style, but there are other times when I prefer to focus on the other important stuff in my business, so appoint a man to act for me. You have to pick your battles in life and I am never one for doing things the hard way if there is an easier way!

a funny - or not so funny - story!

My staff are fantastic at shielding me from unwanted sales calls. A few years ago a sales guy had phoned and phoned. It seemed as though he was never going to give up. One day I was standing by the workstation of one of the team when he called in. Feeling sorry for my team and conscious of how time-consuming his incessant calls were, I said I would take the call. So my member of staff said to him, 'You're in luck, our MD is here today, I'll put you through to her,' at which point he said 'What! Your MD is as women? Don't bother then!' and he put the phone down. We never heard from him again!

There's a great book called *Work With Me: How gender intelligence can help you succeed.* Its written by John Gray and Barbara Annis. I recommend you buy it. But while you are thinking about making that purchase, here is a tiny snippet. It relates to women and men working together (I have experienced a similar situation of frustrating mis-communication during unsuccessful business negotiations):

We're at an impasse when women don't realise that men's actions are not intentionally dismissive. And men don't notice how their behaviours, so much a part of the male dominated corporate culture, cause women to feel that their ideas are disregarded. Men simply don't understand and appreciate the unique value that women bring to the table and women don't know how to frame the conversation in ways that men can relate to and act upon.

CHAPTER THREE

how much will you risk?

> The difference between employment and entrepreneurship is not the capital, the brain power or the idea. No. It's just the ability to take the risk by deciding to leave your comfort zone and move to the unknown.
>
> Bichachi

We talked earlier about what it is that you want in business. Another obvious question is 'How much will you risk?'

Understanding your own risk profile before you head out into the business world is important.

When talking to the clients of my Human Resources consultancy about their attitude to business risk in managing their staff, I ask to what degree they would choose to stay on the right side of employment legislation and avoid being taken to a tribunal. This is the analogy I put to them:

As you enter into a town the speed limit changes from 60 miles per hour to 30 miles per hour. As a business do you:

- reduce to 28 mph in order to be well within the speed limit?
- reduce to 30 mph so you are driving on the speed limit?
- reduce to 35 mph as you consider there to be a low risk of being caught and penalised?
- reduce to 40 as the risk is acceptable and the penalty affordable if you are caught?
- not reduce at all, as getting to your destination is more important than laws and regulations and if you are caught, you know and accept that it will cost you dear?

Over my seventeen years of being in business, I have had clients right across this spectrum. Each business has its own culture and often that culture will determine its attitude to risk. There is no right or wrong stance to take on risk, it just has to be a stance that you are comfortable with.

And you need to decide what your personal risk profile in business is as this will help you make decisions along the way. Consider your attitude to taking risks with:

1. money
2. leaving a financially secure job to start up a business
3. leaving what makes you feel safe (being a mother, working for someone else etc.) and risking your self-confidence by entering into new territory
4. venturing with your business into new untested markets
5. stepping away from the normal and expected by running
6. a business that is different to anything any of your friends and family do
7. your relationships with family and friends if they view you as too ambitious or not doing what they approve of.

To create a gauge for yourself, indicate on a scale of 1-10 on each of these areas of risk:

Your risk profile: 1= prefers low risk; 10 = comfortable with high risk

1. Money

⟵──────────────────⟶

2. Leaving a financially secure job to start up a business

⟵──────────────────⟶

3. Leaving what makes you feel safe

⟵──────────────────⟶

4. Taking your business into untested markets

⟵──────────────────⟶

5. Stepping away from the normal and expected

⟵──────────────────⟶

6. Doing something your friends and family might disapprove of

⟵──────────────────⟶

Becoming an entrepreneur is inherently risky. There is no corporate organisation covering your back. There are no guarantees of success. You cannot control the marketplace and you cannot control the global economy with its ups and downs. If you fear all types of risk then becoming an entrepreneur may just result in too much stress for you.

However, if you are a little risk-averse, but not totally allergic to it, you can limit your risks in business.

With legislation and regulations you can decide that you will always drive at 30 in a 30 mph speed zone. You then manage your finances, your legal compliance issues, your staffing, your suppliers etc., all with a view to doing precisely what the law or regulations require.

With suppliers, you check them out before you sign any contracts, you pay little or nothing up front, you check references, you have good opt-out clauses, you require them to demonstrate they are insured, you spread any risk across a number of suppliers rather than giving a whopping great contract to just one supplier.

With finances you can limit risk by growing organically (i.e. only growing at the speed at which you can fund that from the business) rather than seeking out an external investor or external financing to grow quickly. You put in place strict credit control procedures so you don't go bust waiting for people to pay you. You have tight contracts with suppliers. You forge good links with your bank. You have more than one client so you are never too exposed to losing your whole business if one customer leaves you. You remind yourself daily that cash flow is everything. You can make all the profit in the world but if you mess up with cash flow you will go bust so you get cash flow forecasts, you do your accounts properly at least once every month and you keep on top of your finances daily.

But remember – entrepreneurship is a roller-coaster. It is full of thrills and spills. Risk can be fun. So don't so over protect yourself and your business that you take all the fun and adventure out of the ride.

and what about the risk profile of others?

Whilst you may now have a clear picture of your own risk profile, chances are it may well be higher than the risk profile of the people you subsequently employ. I never thought this would be a problem given that I was the boss and my team were the employees, but from time to time, I have to admit, it has been.

Over the years I have suggested that the business follow certain strategies or enter into new markets. For me, each time I proposed something new, I accepted that there was a possibility of failure. But without a little risk, for me, you take the fun out of the business and I don't want a life time of bland, boring with no change or adventure. But if your staff fear the risk, rather than get excited by the risk, they can scupper your ideas by not 'buying in' and at times, they will even work against you.

In fact, in extreme cases, their negativity and refusal to buy in could scupper your whole business if you let it. Never underestimate the fear of risk and the determination of many to maintain the status quo.

It took me a long time to understand that my risk profile was significantly higher than that of most of the people I employed, and that I had to take account of their fears when making decisions and deciding strategy. After all, I couldn't achieve what I wanted to achieve without them.

So I would encourage you to not only know your own risk profile, but to also consider the risk profile of those around you. In this way you can plan how to introduce new ideas and products in such a way that you keep those around you on board with your ideas, rather than fighting tooth and nail to maintain the status quo.

CHAPTER FOUR

what's in a name?

The best piece of advice I got when setting up my first business was to avoid using my own name as a company name. Names rarely stand out. They can also often appear quite egotistical. They won't be so obvious when people search for the company on the internet and if you have a common surname you might find you will never achieve anything in respect of search engine listings. But most importantly, for me I feel that choosing a name is part of creating an identity. The identity then leads to the branding, website design marketing literature and even your corporate values.

I am sure you can think of a few names that have worked (Ben & Jerry's, Disney, Selfridges, Ford, Dyson, Rowntree etc.) but it's not a route I would advise.

> During the first fourteen years of running my business my name was Helen Clarke. For many of those years the prime minister of New Zealand was Helen Clark. Had my company been named after me, potential clients would have only found me after scrolling through many pages on Google as 'Helen Clark' occupied so much space. Be careful if you use your own name for your business.

The name I chose for my first company was Quintox. It was a name that meant nothing in particular, but it stood out and was a bit different.

Others choose a name that identifies what their business does. Perhaps that is a more practical approach, but it doesn't always give your business identity a sense of buzz and uniqueness.

Others yet choose words that have some hidden or long-forgotten meaning. I have mixed views on these. Some choose religious references, or use ancient languages such as Latin. This approach often helps to convey a sense of education or higher purpose and sometimes they add 'gravitas' to the business. However, they can sound a bit empty at times, a bit overused and if no one understands what you are referring to, then have you achieved what you wanted to achieve? How many teenagers (and adults) for example have a clue that Nike was the Greek Goddess of Victory? I won't deny that Nike is a successful global brand, but how many around the world actually understand the link between the Company name and victory?

Then there are those business names that once meant something but now no one has a clue what they mean: FPL engineering, PB Education, FN Trading Group, COB IT, HNNJ and Co, MWC Ltd, GWDT Group. I'm afraid I am a human with a multitude of things on my desk at any one time. How am I supposed to remember how to spell their name when next I want to find them on the net or send them an email? With names like these I instantly admit defeat. I know it's my failing, but my memory in a busy world just isn't good enough.

One of my current companies is called Jaluch. We named that in a hurry and in ten years it has never quite worked. But how do you change a name when you are already trading? That is really tough, so for now, we are stuck with it.

And what doesn't work about Jaluch? Well, people struggle to pronounce and spell it. That makes them feel uncomfortable and embarrassed at times, which isn't a great way to start a conversation with someone who might become our next client. And when they can't spell it, then they struggle to send us emails or find us on the net. That's not great for either marketing or smooth and easy client relations.

But looking at names that stand out, but that don't come from either Latin or their owners' own names, well there are a few that immediately come to mind: Virgin, Apple, Jaguar and Sky. All of them are easy to remember; company names like these tend to be visual, often using words that convey some sort of meaning about the product. For me, I get this sense from the different companies: different and daring (Virgin), sleek and fast (Jaguar), creative and unexpected (Apple) and imaginative and pushing boundaries (Sky).

If you haven't read it yet you might be interested to read the Steve Jobs' biography which was written by Walter Isaacson. It's a fascinating book on many counts. But in it there is detailed information about how the name Apple came about. One of their chief concerns was that they wanted a computer name that stood out from the computer crowd. It also reflected the fact that Jobs at the time was going through his fruitarian phase and had also just been working on an apple farm, so clearly apples were uppermost in his mind! Did you know that originally the bite taken out of the apple in the logo was a silhouette of Jobs' face?

When choosing your company name, don't rush it and don't force it. Mull over ideas, let them evolve, get people on board who have creative brains who can help. Your company name could be around for a hundred years or more so give it some respect and don't rush the process (like I did!).

a cautionary tale ...

As I have said, my first business was called Quintox. I sold it after five years but was able to get the trading name back around six months later. When I first set the business up, the word Quintox was just a made-up word. It meant nothing and no-one else in the world had a company name that was similar. However when I got the name back shortly after setting up Jaluch, by chance, I checked on the internet to see if anyone was trading under the Quintox name. They were. All over the search engines were references to a mouse and rat poison called Quintox. Given that I was in the HR industry, I took the decision never to re-use the name Quintox even though I now legally could. It was a narrow escape and I have no idea why I decided to check for other companies on Google using the name Quintox. But I'm glad I did!

CHAPTER FIVE

branding

This chapter looks at various aspects of branding – creating your business brand, corporate values, product brands and personal brands.

As with naming your business, you need to take care with branding your business as the decisions you make now about branding may well stay with you for years.

But before I head into a few tips and guidance on creating your own business brand I thought I would ask you to start thinking about some of the brands you will be familiar with already. Think about how these businesses are branded, whether you like or dislike their branding, how they advertise their brand, what their brand says about what they sell, what their brand says about their customers, what these brands do right, and in some instances, what these brands do wrong.

A few brands for you to think about:

Swarowski

McDonalds

Dell

Harrods

Disney

creating your business brand

Once you have your business name then you can start to create your brand. This is a whole book in itself so here are just a few hints and tips, but first a few words on consistency:

consistency is key

How companies can damage their own brands.

A bank – I have been a business customer of this particular bank for years and I am really familiar with their internet banking and their branches. I don't really need to write to them much and equally hardly ever receive any letters. One day, though, a letter came through about a business transaction. I was astonished. The letter looked like it had been produced in the 1960s, the font, branding, style and language was all out of synch with the branding I saw on a daily basis on its website. It looked awful. I felt that it showed a business that wasn't 'joined up' in the way it created its image and delivered its service. Front end of the business looks great. Back end of the business, still in the dark ages.

A legal firm – this firm of solicitors operates out of swish new offices. It has a modern image in the press, tells us it is a business that is going places. But consistently over my time of using them they send me letters in the post. I email them with a question, then three to five days later a letter arrives in the post. Their communication style is out of synch with their branding and I feel as though they don't deliver what their company branding suggests to me that they will deliver. Essentially I feel let down, disappointed and, to a degree, duped. Again, this is an example of the front end of the business looking great, but the back end of the business still in the dark ages.

Often the following will make up the business brand:

- your logo and strapline
- your website and marketing literature (words, images used, style, tone, translation options etc.)
- the style and nature of your business blogs and tweets
- the words you use to describe your business on LinkedIn or Facebook
- the style and feel of business documents
- the way you and your staff look (and sometimes the vehicles you drive)
- your product packaging
- your customer care approach/policy.

There are many, many things that go into creating your brand but hopefully I have covered the critical ones.

But now just a few tips and ideas on creating your brand ...

Thinking it through:

- Don't rush it; let ideas evolve.
- Find ten brands relating to products or services. Choose five that you love and five that you hate. Try to work out what it is about the ones you love and what it is about the ones you hate. If at any point you work with a graphic designer I would suggest you show them these ten brands to help explain what you do and do not like.
- What do you want your brand message to say about your business? Think about things such as fun, serious, traditional, reliable, innovative, cutting edge, no frills, ethical, intellectual, international, local, high integrity, risky and challenging, considerate, value driven, community driven, safe, futuristic etc.
- Do you want words and an image to form your logo or just words (i.e. the name of your business)?

- Do you want to build a brand that in due course becomes as valuable in the market as the products or services you actually sell?

Creating the brand:

- Whom do you want to receive your message, and is your brand targeted correctly for this group?
- Are you going to bodge this job so you are good to go, spend enough time to make it fit for purpose, or are you going to employ an expert to make it absolutely perfect?
- Can you decide on a few easy things such as colour, font, logo, values, then let the brand evolve over time, or do you want to spend some serious time creating your brand in full before you start?
- Is there a danger you will spend so much time sorting the brand that you will never launch your business?

Reviewing and perfecting:

- When you have created your brand, look hard at it. Critique it.
- Decide if it is something that you can live with for the next ten years. If it isn't, go back to the drawing board.
- Consider whether it is going to do the job you want and need it to do. If it isn't, go back to the drawing board.
- And finally decide whether it excites you and fills you with enthusiasm. If it doesn't, then again you need to go back to that drawing board!

> If you could choose one word to describe the brand you want to create or have created, what would it be?

values

A critical part of your thinking about business branding might include deciding on the values your enterprise will have. If you don't know where to start with this, check the internet for 'corporate values' to get a feel for what others are using. You might also take some time to think about your personal values.

My personal values have always been reflected in the way I run my business. This doesn't have to be the case, but taking half an hour to think through your own values might help you focus.

Write here your personal values:

NOTES

When I first wrote my business values, there were eight of them. In hindsight that was far too many and in recent years I have always stuck to three. Three is manageable and means that they can be easily incorporated into websites, blogs, staff documents and marketing materials etc. My current corporate values are Courage, Care and Commitment.

I think these values say something about me and the type of client service I wish to deliver. However, it's been interesting that asking my team to be courageous has not always been easy. You can't force people to be courageous and also what feels courageous to others, might not feel courageous to you (and vice versa of course). I suppose what I am saying is: choose your values carefully. For you to run your business every day in line with your values, and to manage your staff in line with your values, you have got to totally believe in them and be committed to them. Unless of course you are choosing some values as a PR exercise only.

It may be that you don't really want to live and breathe any values, but you feel there is a need to create some as the world expects it of you and they can be useful padding in corporate statements such as press releases or home pages of websites. If this is the case, can I make a plea? If I could be given a pair of earrings for every time I have seen a company tell me that one of their corporate values is 'integrity', my jewellery box would be overflowing. I have seen 'integrity' used by airlines, banks, consultants, retailers, estate agents and a myriad of others. Integrity is in fact a word that could mean so much about a business, but it is in fact often just rolled out as a value by those who appear to have no real values at all. So my plea is 'please don't do it!' However, it is always your choice so if you do use 'integrity' as one of your values, then be clear about what you are doing, why you are doing it and how it might expose you to (unspoken) criticism.

values and recruitment

The recruitment and management of staff is an ongoing challenge for entrepreneurs, but not necessarily in the start-up phase. Whilst I am talking about values, I want to say a few words about recruitment as some of you will already be recruiting and managing staff.

Traditionalists would say that when you want to recruit, you identify what skills and experience you need to add into the business; you then write an advert around that and then recruit to fill the gap. Traditionalists, though, often don't have their own money and energy invested in the enterprise. Increasing numbers of entrepreneurs I know recruit their core team on the basis of shared values, rather than perfect skill or experience fit.

You can always develop skills and provide experience, but you can seldom change people's values. So if values are important to you, put them on your website, include them in your job ads, talk about them at interview and crucially, find a way to check that the personal values your job candidates tell you they have are in fact their genuine values, rather than something fabricated for this interview.

Instead of questions such as 'What are your personal values?', instead ask: 'One of our corporate values is commitment. Can you take five minutes to talk me through what you understand by the value "commitment" and give me an example of a specific situation in your current role where you have demonstrated real commitment at work?'

> 'No wriggle room.' When seeking specific answers to important questions, don't give your candidates room to wriggle, waffle or go off on a tangent. Keep your questions focused and specific to ensure that you get out of your interviews the information you need.

But before you get to interview them, you have to find a way of attracting in the right candidates who will demonstrate the right values and so help you to live and breathe your values as you grow your business. What do you think of the two different styles of job ads I have set out below, assuming you want to add a PA to your team? The first focuses on skills and experience; the second focuses on behaviours and values. Same job though!

personal assistant required

Must be IT literate and experienced in the use of Word, Excel, Webex, PowerPoint and Survey Monkey.

Duties include organising conferences, travel, diary management and day to day support for the MD of this busy company.

3-5 years experience preferred. Must have excellent grasp of spelling and grammar, and numeracy is essential.

3 days per week. Good references required.

To apply please send cv and covering letter to ...

personal assistant sought

We are a fast-growing and busy team and looking for someone to join us to help us deliver a fantastic service for our clients.

We value people in the team who can get things done, people who embrace new technology and who bring to the workplace a really positive attitude. People who want to commit to our growth and enjoy sharing our successes.

If you have good personal assistant skills and experience and great references and would enjoy activities such as conference and travel organisation, then call us today to find out more and tell us a little about why you think you would be a good cultural fit for us.

As with the job ads to the left, what I want to help you do is understand that sometimes there is a hard way and an easy way to do things in business. Many of us have learnt things the hard way, but I'm hoping that you won't have to!

In this case, don't waste money and effort sifting through useless CVs when you could change the style of your job ad to achieve better quality applicants. Equally don't waste three months employing someone who is a total cultural misfit just because they ticked all the boxes in your job ad. You don't have enough energy or time when setting up in business to waste on managing cultural misfits.

> You can always develop skill sets, but you can't change people's values or attitude, so recruit for values and attitude and then aim to develop skills.

But then, perhaps I am preaching to the converted, as being an entrepreneur is often about finding new ways to do things, of not necessarily following the pack and mimicking what others do, of having the confidence to do it your way. Are you there yet, or perhaps a 'work in progress'?

> Did you know that when someone under twenty-five sets up in business that they dramatically increase their chances of success in the first few years if they set up with a business partner aged over thirty? If the under-twenty-fives are aware of this from the outset, then hopefully they will be encouraged to take the necessary steps to increase their chances of success.

When setting up, whatever our age, we don't always know there is an easier way to do things. That's because often at the start we don't ask enough questions, meet enough business people, have good networks with the people who could help, or we are too self-sufficient and independent to recognise the value of other people's experience.

And it's not necessarily about taking advice from others. It's more about hearing a wealth of experiences, putting all those into our heads to churn over and reflect on and then distilling out the learning points that are relevant for us.

The easier way to do things in business when starting out is to invest time in learning from others who have 'been there, done that'! And to give you a head start in this process why not read the mini case studies later on in this book which come from a whole variety of my contacts in my network who wanted to share their experiences with you.

and now, a task for you:

Over the next week, everywhere you go, every piece of corporate literature you read, see what they say about their values. Collect all their statements together and take some time to think about which ones you like and which ones you don't like.

product branding

As well as the corporate brand, businesses also have product brands. This could relate to just one product or service, or to a range.

In an ideal world, if you are creating a product brand, its branding will be consistent with your corporate branding. Creating something that is inconsistent will send confused messages to your clients about your branding generally.

A great example of a product brand that worked well for me was a jewellery and accessories company that had one of its values as 'ethical'. In its corporate literature and on its website it talked about its ethical approach to business and its desire to only create products from recycled materials: wood, metals, precious stones, beads etc. One Christmas they launched a giftware range of small wooden carvings for stocking fillers that children could buy for their parents. The product range was called 'driftwood'. A new range and new products, but entirely in line with their corporate branding.

I find that lots of small companies have a company name and company branding, but they never take the time to create product branding. But it can be fun if you do this and it can say so much about what your organisation is about.

A business contact was selling goods that were all ethically sourced. It has always been one of her personal values to seek to recycle or only use materials that come from sustainable sources. She told me one day that when she told a woman who was buying from her that everything she sold was ethically sourced, the woman added extra items to her shopping basket. When we later discussed this, my business contact said that she didn't want to include her values on her product branding as she wanted people to buy because they loved her products and designs and not because they were made from ethically sourced materials. I urged her to rethink her product branding, but I don't think she has.

creating a personal brand

A woman recently followed me on Twitter. This is how she had worded her 'profile': 'Wife, mother, marketing geek and generally nice person who teaches fun loving business owners how to get new customers.'

What do you think of her personal brand?

After I 'followed her back' she then sent me a direct message: 'Visit my Facebook page to get my five tips on how to sell to new customers.'

I didn't visit her Facebook page. So why didn't I think her five tips would be of value to me? The answer is that she hadn't convinced me she could sell herself, let alone give advice on how to sell to others. Her personal branding – as interpreted by me (and I recognise that everyone could interpret it differently) – told me that:

- ❖ Her work would always come second to her numerous family commitments.
- ❖ More than anything, she loves being a geek (which doesn't give me enormous confidence that she has the excellent people skills I might expect of someone selling sales expertise).
- ❖ She sees herself as 'generally nice' even though 'nice' is a pretty bland word that might describe someone who is not a strong character, who is probably no more than 'average' and who is more of a team player than decision-maker or business driver.
- ❖ She thinks she can be so choosy as to stipulate she only wants to work with fun business owners. Does she think all business is just fun? Or perhaps she views her business as just a bit of fun? Either way, you might wonder if she is going to take the business of helping you get new sales leads seriously enough.
- ❖ She says she is a marketing geek, but then offers sales tips. Is she a marketing or sales expert or does she not differentiate between the two?

The reality of course is that she might be great at what she does, but her personal branding was such that I will never get to find out.
Have I been too harsh? I might have been, but first impressions really count so you need to really think through how you describe yourself to others.

Ten years ago the concept of the personal brand wasn't really discussed in business circles. Of course there were celebrities who had their personal brand, but in the business world, few company owners even thought about creating one.

However, in recent years, partly in response to the growth of the internet and increasing use of social media channels for communication, personal branding has become a huge phenomenon. In the UK obvious business examples of this are Lord Sugar, Peter Jones and Richard Branson. Prince Charles is another example. Thanks to their personal branding, we know a bit about what these people like and don't like and what some of their passions in life are, irrespective of how well we know their companies.

Its embarrassing though that I can't really think of many examples of female business leaders in my own country who have a strong personal brand. There are of course dozens of models, singers, actresses, and TV celebrities who have ventured into the business world, but for the most part their branding is not appropriate to mimic if you want people to take you seriously and be more interested in your skills than how you look.

Can you identify three business women in the public eye who have strong personal brands? List them here and alongside each name summarise what their brand is, what it says about them and what you most like or dislike about their brands.

There is a reason though, why so few female business leaders have strong personal brands. In essence modesty is still expected of women in most societies, whatever their role or level in society and women who demonstrate a lack of modesty by 'parading their successes in public' often find themselves subject to sanctions as a result.

However, just as female employees hold back their own careers in the workplace by not asking for promotions or pay rises, in the business world, female business owners inhibit the growth of their own businesses by not trumpeting their business successes.

It really is so hard to strike the right balance as a female business owner. To be ambitious, but not too ambitious; to be assertive, but not to the point of being considered aggressive; and to be successful, but not so much that you are viewed as egotistical and lacking the necessary feminine 'bashfulness'. It's a real challenge, but you will have to find a way to balance the need to publicise yourself and your business, in order to achieve the business growth you want, versus your desire to hold back in order to not attract criticism.

If you want to learn more about this challenge of striking the right balance, lots of research has been published. A fascinating read is Why Women Don't Ask by Sara Laschever and Linda Babcock and the following is an extract from a research paper from INSEAD:

* scan me

> In experiment after experiment, women who achieve in distinctly male arenas are seen as competent, but are less well liked than equally successful men (Heilman, Wallen, Fuchs, & Tamkins, 2004:416). Merely being a successful woman in a male domain can be regarded as a violation of gender norms warranting sanctions (e.g. Heilman & Okimoto, 2000). By the same token, when women performing traditionally male roles are seen as conforming to feminine stereotypes, they tend to be liked, but not respected (Rudman &Glick, 2001: 744) they are judged too soft, emotional, and unassertive to make tough decisions and to come across as sufficiently authoritative (Eagly &Carly, 2007). In short, women can face trade offs between competence and likeability in leadership roles.
>
> Insead 2011 Faculty and research working paper: 'Taking gender into account: theory and deign for women's leadership development programmes'

> If you were to set up a profile on Linkedin tomorrow how would you summarise your interests and strengths?

But returning to the issue of personal branding, if you are setting up a business in today's environment, I do think you will need to consider whether there could be a business benefit in creating a personal brand. It is widely accepted that business growth in the current economic environment is most easily achieved through networking, referrals and social media channels. All of these of course, rely on business owners being highly visible – however uncomfortable that may feel. I do recognise, though, that in some cultures personal branding by female business owners will not be accepted for many years to come and you should never jeopardise your own safety and well being just because the international business community says a personal brand is important.

CHAPTER SIX

business planning

This chapter provides just a short insight into business planning. There are whole books that cover this topic, and business coaches galore who would love to spend three days or even three weeks guiding you through.

It may surprise you but I know of business owners who are running multi-million-pound businesses without a business plan in place. For my part, I am sure I didn't have one in the early years of running my business as I had such a relaxed laissez faire approach to many things in those early days, but I have certainly had a business plan for many years now and would recommend you do too.

Interesting fact: Only 31% of new business owners set up with a business plan in place.

why plan and why so few have a plan?

If you are booking a holiday there are certain things you do. You work out how much money you have, you think about where you want to go, when you want to go and how long you will stay for. You consider what accommodation

Then, before you get on the plane, you work through what needs to be done to actually get away on holiday: what clothes you need, how much currency to order, how you will get to the airport, what jabs you need to protect you from nasty diseases, care arrangements for your dog or cat and possibly also your mother, and inevitably you write a list for packing to ensure nothing is forgotten or missed. For most holidays there is a lot of planning involved. And women are often good at the planning. Thinking it through is one of the natural skills for many of us. We might even be accused by men at times of over thinking and over-planning and they wouldn't be wrong!

> I used this quote before and I don't apologise for using it again here as this point is critical if you want to be a professional business owner: 'if you don't know where you are going how will you know when you get there?'

So why then do so few women prepare a business plan before they set up their enterprise? You have to admit it's a bit odd! But as I said earlier, I even know businesses that have been trading for years and they still don't have a business plan or strategy document in place.

The business plan is like your holiday packing and preparation guide and your holiday itinerary guide all rolled into one. It's your way of ensuring that your business has the best chance possible of succeeding and growing.

I have some thoughts, though, as to why so many business owners do not have a plan. If I could hazard a guess, this failure to create a plan is for one or more of the following reasons:

skills and knowledge

- ❖ They don't really know what a business plan looks like and don't know how to create one.

- They are embarrassed by their lack of business knowledge, understanding of business terminology and their ability to write in a 'business' style so its easier to just not put pen to paper.
- They don't appreciate the complexity of running a business and the enormous juggling act that so often has to be done and that could be simpler if a plan was in place.
- They don't know how to use the computer programs required to create one (e.g. Word and Excel).
- They are dyslexic. Alternatively, they lack essential literacy or numeracy skills and don't like to ask for support.

fear factors and commitment

- A business plan would mean that they have to come out into the open with their family who, up until this point, they have told this is 'just a little hobby, nothing serious'.
- They don't really have any faith in their ability to make this venture successful so they choose to keep it as informal and as low-key as possible.
- Some fear failure, and if you don't write down what your targets are then you will never be in a position of having failed.
- Writing it down might make it look scary.
- An allergy to admin!
- They are, quite simply, lazy!

Business planning isn't rocket science, though, and if you are not accessing external funding, no one needs to see the end result but you.

For me, if you stick to **KISS – Keep it simple and straightforward**, you should do fine.

what goes into a business plan

Just as a simple checklist for a business that is in its infancy, here is what I think you might look to include:

- an overview of your business
- some market and competitor analysis
- about your organisation – vision, values, structure, unique selling points, management, ownership etc.
- a summary of your products/services
- your business strategy – including pricing strategy, target market, distribution/sales strategy, marketing strategy
- an analysis of your financials including sales, profit and cash flow forecasts.

a sample plan

You can find sample business plans in lots of places if you search on the net, but at the end of this section I have given you an example of the business plan format that I have used for many years.

Perhaps my very simple format could be a starting point for you. It fits one A4 page of paper and each year I update it to keep me focused. I have seen businesses that create plans that fill whole lever-arch files; a silly waste of time in my opinion, given the speed at which business priorities and needs change and the fact that no-one ever re-reads them across the year. I re-read mine often, and usually share it with my team at our monthly team meetings. You can do that quite easily when there is just one page.

What I do is set out on the left and right hand sides of the page some of the critical numbers for my business for the financial year just ending (left hand side) and the financial year just starting (right hand side).

I run an HR and training consultancy so for me the categories include:

- sales
- costs
- profit
- new client sales
- customer care visits
- web hits
- blog hits
- number of training days delivered
- average price of a training day
- HR advice hours billed
- average price of an hour billed
- team productivity average.

Then in the middle of the page I have four lines, each containing about eight activity boxes. In these I write in what we are seeking to do. Keeping track of what we actually do is easy, as each month I just turn the box purple if we have completed it.

My top line usually relates to **strategic** actions. This year one of our actions has been around diversifying our product base and setting up an e-commerce store to sell our training products.

The second line relates to some of the key **business development** activities. One of these this year has been to dramatically overhaul the fortnightly emails we send to clients, as sales enquiries following our emails have been dropping off.

The third line relates to **delivering our services** – namely HR advice and training. One of the activities in this line we have this year is to review the training materials we currently use to ensure consistency and quality.

And the fourth line relates to what you might call **'back office' activities**. These are the activities that are essential to keep us operating efficiently and effectively. One of ours for this year was to upgrade both our IT hardware and software, as slow systems and mismatched software were costing us

Keeping the boxes to no more than eight on each line means that you have to be disciplined in what you include and keeps you focussed on the important things that will make a difference in your business. Perhaps if you are a sole trader, though, you ought to aim for just three boxes on each line as you have to be realistic about what just one person can achieve.

Vision and Values – I don't start my plan with the vision and values, as we talk about these constantly within the business, but some people like to include their vision and values in their business plan. Include yours if that suits you.

Target market – I also don't include details of our target market as again, these are well defined within the business and we discuss them often. If it provides clarity for you, then include your target market within your business plan.

The money! – Sitting behind my one-page business plan I always have a one-page spreadsheet that contains all the numbers! Nothing overly complex because I hate that, but a spreadsheet that shows on one page, month by month, the projected sales, costs and profit for the financial year. If you don't yet know how to create a spreadsheet with some really simple formulas in, then I recommend that now is the time you learn. And on your list of skills to learn – I would consider this a 'need to have' not 'nice to have'.

> If money issues really do concern you and for whatever reason you do not want to attend an open (public) workshop, then here is a link to an opportunity for one to one coaching in business planning and finances.

Finally, just a little word on optimism versus pessimism in your plans. I think my team would agree that I have a tendency to optimism when putting the plan together. It gives me a nice feeling to have something to strive towards but I know that it can be demotivating to others if the targets seem out of reach, so I do try to rein my optimism in a bit. On the flip side, if you have a tendency to pessimism then be aware of that and try to make your goals a little more stretching.

business planning | 95

Key measurements year ending April 2013		strategy					Key measurements year ending April 2014
Turnover	Product/service diversification - establish e commerce site for training product						
Cost							
Profit							
		business development					
New av sales per month							
Customer care visits av per month			Re-develop fortnightly emails to generate more sales enquiries				
Website traffic av per month							
		service/product delivery					
Blog hits av per month							
Break even on training	review training materials to ensure consistency and quality						
Av days delivered per month							
		business support					
					Office software/ hardware upgrade		

succeeding in business

When I started out in business, the scaremongers suggested that as many as 50% of new businesses fail within the first year. Recently I have seen lower figures suggested, and I think the prevailing view is that start-ups have about a 60% chance of surviving three years and a 50% chance of surviving five years. So the odds are looking better!

There are, of course, numerous reasons why businesses fail, some of which will be within your control and some of which will not. But there are many things that you can do to increase your chances of succeeding in business. But these need to be done from the outset.

These are some of the great things I have seen start-up owners do – which of these do you think you should make a priority?

clarity of vision/purpose

- ❖ Be clear (and honest with yourself) about why you are setting up and what you want from your business venture.
- ❖ Be honest with yourself about how much money you have to invest and how much money you need out of the business to survive during the first twelve to twenty-four months.
- ❖ Set yourself some clear targets for six, twelve, eighteen and twenty-four months so you know exactly where you are headed.

support

- ❖ Get a mentor and properly use them right from the start.
- ❖ Get your family on board with your plans and deal with, rather than ignore, any signs of discontent.
- ❖ Identify anyone in your inner circle who is likely to dent your confidence or undermine you and take steps to remove them from the inner circle.

- Involve fully and from the outset someone with solid experience of running a business; bring them in either as a non-executive director, partner, fellow director.

business management

- Cut corners with the stuff that doesn't matter, but don't cut any corners with critical things that could impact your ability to sell or deliver.
- Implement from day one essential processes and procedures to manage cash flow and sales.

strategic planning

- Put time aside to do proper research, thinking and planning before you invest money and actually set up your business.
- Create a plan for your own personal development and set aside some time and money to formally develop your skills. So many women, I find, view this as a luxury rather than a necessity.
- Identify what skill and experience gaps you have and put a plan in place to involve – and eventually recruit – people who do have these skills and experience.
- Be disciplined enough to ensure that every single month you have time away from the day to day business to properly think about the business.

> Did you know ... that during an economic downturn it has been estimated that 50% fewer female-owned business than male-owned businesses go into liquidation? This is often thought to be down to the fact that women tend to grow their businesses organically (often not accessing external funding) and more cautiously.

CHAPTER SEVEN

running your business

In this chapter we look at few of the critical areas involved in running your young business. I suggest that you just read those sections that you are interested in at this time.

the tedious admin

I recently came across a business that has a wonderful product. They operate in the giftware industry and currently distribute their products to a huge number of gift shops in museums, galleries, leisure parks and holiday centres. At first glance you might think that there is nothing that is going to stop that business from achieving great success. But in my view they could well go bust.

Perhaps tomorrow, perhaps next week or perhaps next year. And why do I think this? Well the two business owners are really artistic and creative. They love creating new gift items, coming up with designs, creating their fantastic website, having brainstorming sessions with their small production team and creating new marketing fliers. But the business lacks infrastructure. . It lacks processes, procedures, management information, paperwork and structure. Just as one example, I know that they have already been late with numerous orders, ended up selling one item at about £1 less than it cost them to make it and twice they have gone right to the wire (financially) as they hadn't been keeping up with both their invoicing and credit control activities.

It's the equivalent of having a sweet shop with all you have made in full view of the street, looking wonderful, but when that product is sold, you have no idea about who bought it, at what price, what needs restocking, when it needs restocking, what you have banked and what you have spent buying new materials, what you paid your staff to help you sell it, and what your landlord is going to ask you for rent in three days' time.

It's just not a sustainable way to run a business and you really need to be organised from day one. You don't need sophisticated systems and processes and you certainly don't need to go out and buy some expensive, complex CRM (customer relationship management) or stock management software; just something that is simple and easy to use and above all, fit for purpose.

I am not an advocate ever of processes and procedures just for the sake of it, but processes and procedures are great at keeping you on track. You can land the order of the century, but if your business lacks the infrastructure to be able to deliver on that order, then your business will fail.

At all times, you need to know essential information such as:

customers

- ❖ Who your customers are, what they buy from you, at what price and how often.
- ❖ What your customers think of you, how they can complain to you and how you deal with their complaints.
- ❖ How new customers will find you or come to you.

suppliers

- ❖ What your suppliers are charging you and how this compares to last week and last year.
- ❖ Whether your suppliers are working in partnership with your business or view you as just an organisation to sell something to whenever they get the opportunity.

staff

- What your staff are doing during the day and whether time is being spent doing the right things.
- Whether your staff attend work often enough for you to make a profit (i.e. are you on top of staff attendance and staff absence?).
- Whether your staff have the skills and the right attitude to help you achieve business success (you might read the book Fish; a remarkable way to boost morale and improve results if you are interested in ensuring your staff come to work with the right attitude).
- What your staff are costing you each month.
- How your business will be exposed if key staff leave and how you can bridge the gap.

finances

- What is currently in the bank, what is owed to you, and what you need to pay out.
- What your monthly and annual overheads are.
- What the profit margin on each of your services/products is.
- What you need to achieve each month to break even and then make a profit.
- What the gap will be between invoicing and you being paid and how you will cover that gap.

sales

- What sales you are losing, or what clients do not buy again from you and why.
- What sales, if any, are loss leaders. Equally, what sales always give you a great profit margin.
- What your target sales are and how you are doing against those targets.

competitors

- What your competitors are doing.
- How your prices compare.
- How your offering compares.
- How they are innovating and changing.
- What sets you apart – what your USPs (unique selling points) are.

business continuity

- What you will do if your internet connection, website (or telephone system) goes down for five days (or even one day!).
- Where your information is backed up and how long it will take to restore if your server is burnt out in an office fire or your IT provider goes bust.
- Who will pay your suppliers and staff if you get run over by a bus (i.e. who has the legal authorisation to carry on the business in your absence).
- What you will do if your most important customer goes bust or moves their custom to another supplier.

When you start your business, much of the information you need can be kept on Excel spreadsheets or similar. If you don't have the skills to be able to set up and use spreadsheets then I would suggest this is absolutely critical training for you in the weeks/months running up to launching your business. And don't even think of keeping paper records!

Perhaps you are worried because you never did well with numbers at school? There are many business owners who didn't do well at maths at school; however, this should not preclude you from learning how to set up spreadsheets and being able to input essential information. Sometimes it is much easier when there is no-one looking over your shoulder hassling you to come up with the right answer, and sometimes it is much easier when you can see the point of what you are trying to do, when the numbers start to mean something.

If you suffer from dyslexia, though, and that impacts on your ability to be confident with numbers, then make sure that in your group of supporters and those who help you, there are people working alongside you who can help with this.

But whatever you do, know that you cannot afford to not set up spreadsheets, as having and managing information within your business is absolutely essential.

On the other hand, you should not go overboard with management information and business processes and procedures. Making your business too complicated will do nothing for its profitability and your ongoing success. Think of it as the difference between the procedure manual for an oil tanker versus the procedure manual for an inflatable dinghy. When just starting out, your dinghy really doesn't need anything too sophisticated or complicated, so keep it simple.

And in terms of timing, many like to have a weekly handle on their financial and other information, but monthly is also fine. But, if you are one of those who keep their fingers crossed and only do the books once a year, then prepare yourself for disaster. Once a year is not sensible and is not responsible, so get a handle on your paperwork and don't put if off each month just because it's your least favourite task.

a little story ...

I once knew a business consultant who lost her home because for six months she was so busy supporting her clients and sorting their problems that she never got around to invoicing them. The reality, of course, is that she hated the admin. But what a crazy way to run a business when you need regular money, as we all do in life, in order to pay our essential bills. You might think this woman was unusual. I can assure you she is not. It is simply horrifying how many people fail to do the daily, weekly and monthly admin that is required to keep their business afloat.

outsourcing the jobs you don't know how to do

When you set up your business, it may feel like there are myriad jobs you don't know how to do. The key, though, is not to panic and not to let it overwhelm you.

If you have come from a large company you will have been able to phone someone from maintenance if the light bulb goes, someone from IT if your computer picks up a virus, someone from finance if you have a bill that needs paying, someone from logistics if you need to ship something somewhere, someone from HR if you need a contract for your new recruit, someone from marketing if you want a flier or marketing brochure designed, and someone from compliance if you want to arrange insurance for the exhibition you are about to attend. But when you are running a business, you are on your own – for most things.

The great part of this is that you never have to sit around twiddling your thumbs waiting for someone to come and sort you out! The not so great part is that you have to get on with it or find an external supplier to outsource it to.

Again, when looking at outsourcing, the key to all of this is to keep it simple.

Someone I know has just acquired a business. The business they have acquired has been trading for three years, has four staff and operates out of one office. After acquiring the business, these are some of the things that came out of the woodwork:

- ❖ Finances are outsourced to a finance director who charges £3000 per month to attend for three days per month. This is totally unnecessary for a business of this size and they really shouldn't be spending more than a few hundred pounds per month on bookkeeping support.
- ❖ A leased photocopier on a three-year rolling lease that costs them £7500 per year. Another totally ridiculous overhead and what fantastic sales person talked them into this!

- ❖ A twenty-year lease on the offices they are in with no break clause until they reach six years. Again, this is a massive exposure for a tiny start-up company.

- ❖ A five-year contract with an HR consultancy that provides them with HR support and also legal cover should they be sued. This is costing them £6000 a year for a minimum term of five years and is an incredibly expensive way to get the HR support they need, plus they are protecting at such huge expense against such a tiny employment risk given that only three employees are in a position to ever sue them!

- ❖ A two-year contract with a PR agency to write their blogs, tweet for them and undertake other social media activities at a cost of £2000 per month. Again, this seems a huge commitment for such a new company and what was worse, they had no management processes in place to either see what was being posted on their behalf or measure the return on their investment.

The key is to keep it simple, so don't get sucked into long contracts and don't take out contracts when pay-as-you-go is a far more sensible way to approach things. Also, look around for suppliers rather than accepting the first one who walks through your door, and always negotiate on the lengths of leases.

Interestingly, having learned a bit more about the owner of this business, what occurred to me is that he has a psychometric profile that doesn't like risk. And his massive aversion to risk shows up in the huge overheads he has committed to even though the business is still so young. This risk aversion and failure to use common sense about what is needed, ultimately meant he lost his business and was taken over.

But don't take his miscalculation as a reason not to outsource anything; just be sensible about what you outsource.

Typically I would expect a small business to outsource its monthly bookkeeping, any PR activities it undertakes, some of its design/marketing activities and perhaps also its website and IT support.

tips when looking at suppliers for outsourcing

Tip 1. Are their typical clients the same size as you? If they are all much larger than you then they might have a fee structure that is not appropriate for where you are in business.

Tip 2. What does the small print look like? Is it all about their rights and what they can and cannot do, but leaves no consideration for the fact that you are the customer?

Tip 3. Avoid those who say they only deliver a service under contract. There are plenty of smaller outfits who offer a pay as you go service and this might be better for you in the early days of your business.

Tip 4. Current practice in tendering unfortunately is to include extremely low upfront costs but to say in the small print that virtually every service you might need from them is an extra. These extras then cost a fortune. Don't get stung by the 'extras'.

Tip 5. If the supplier is late for a meeting, fails to send their proposal in or fails to return your phone calls at this early stage of the relationship, then they are probably not going to value you as a customer once you sign on the dotted line.

Tip 6. Does the supplier 'get' your business? Is this someone who shows they understand your business and what you are trying to achieve? Do you think there is any sort of cultural fit between your business and theirs? Don't buy in to a supplier who appears to have no clue or interest in what you do and how you do it.

Tip 7. If their website and literature says that they support small businesses, ask the sales person what that means. This can often just be a marketing/PR statement. Does the sales person actually understand what small businesses need? If not, how will that business actually deliver what you need?

supplier diversity

Many corporates currently talk about supplier diversity. This means that they aim to have a diverse supplier base that reflects the diversity of society. In practice this means actively encouraging suppliers that are female or black and ethnic minority-owned to tender for contracts.

If you are a B2B business you may find that many organisations almost exclusively buy only from male-owned businesses and larger publicly owned businesses. Often, I accept, just because those can be the most dominant in the market.

Interestingly though I have also observed many female owned businesses buying predominantly from male-owned businesses. An interesting business coach I met in Amsterdam recently told me that she had read of research into this. So men don't buy from women and women don't buy from women! Don't be downhearted though as there is a way to crack this cycle ...

Why not, from day one of launching your business, set the standard by having your own supplier diversity policy in place? This means that when seeking quotes from suppliers, always make sure you include one supplier that is female-owned or black/ethnic minority-owned. And to ensure that your supplier diversity policy is working, review your supplier list at least once very six months.

employing and managing staff

Many of you will not immediately employ staff. Perhaps your fledgling business will be just you and your computer. But soon enough you will either be managing staff or managing self-employed workers and associates. So in this section I touch on just a few of the issues around managing staff. Feel free to skip right to the next chapter if this one is not for you.

There are three essential stages in the staff 'lifecycle':

- recruitment
- termination (resignation, retirement, dismissal)
- everything in-between!

recruitment

Another one of you! Often business owners, when seeking to grow their businesses, look to employ someone just like them! In reality this will be a never-ending search and one full of frustrations, as I am sure you will find very quickly that no one else is ever quite as good at the job as you are! So please don't go hunting for another one of you. Instead, why not think about who might complement your skills? As you build your team it will be stronger if it is full of people with different personalities, different experiences and different approaches. Teams that are diverse can be much stronger – provided everyone learns to value what the others bring to the table.

Traditionally businesses have always recruited to a set job description and person specification; however, it is often quoted in business that you 'recruit for skills and experience, but dismiss on behaviour and attitude'. So, if this is the case, how about making your first interview one about behaviour and attitude? Check that your applicants share your corporate values and demonstrate the behaviours needed of someone working in a small start-up business. Flexibility, attitude and great work ethic will probably be essential. You can always train up the skills and provide the experience, but it is exceedingly hard to change someone's behaviours.

If you are still developing confidence in recruiting staff, then you could consider using some psychometric profiles or other assessments during your recruitment process. Many of these are available on line. They won't give you all the answers, but they might help you understand more about the person you are about to offer a job to. If you are interested in this but don't want to commit any money until you know exactly what sort of information you might get from a profile then use this QR code which will take you to a sample psychometric profile.

scan me

In my business we always use psychometric profiles at recruitment. We also often ask candidates to sit a GIA (General Intelligence Assessment). During employment we sometimes use a great tool that assesses emotional intelligence and have used a 360 degree feedback tool during the performance review process. None of these tests will tell you everything about a candidate or person, but they can give you a great insight which can be used in conjunction with any other information you have..

termination

If an employee retires or resigns it is usually pretty straightforward. But if you have to dismiss, then dismissing a member of staff is seldom easy. But putting off dismissing a member of staff who is not performing, or who is misbehaving, will drain your energy and possibly damage your business. When someone is not delivering what you need, you must take action. What I have seen, time after time, is business owners giving members of staff the benefit of the doubt for far too long!

In respect of a newly recruited employee who is not performing, my recommendation is that either you get shot in week one if it is obvious from day one that they are a bad fit, or otherwise you allow about three months to see how they fit into the team, and then aim to make a decision about whether they really should stay with you at around the six-month mark. If you are still undecided at six months, my advice would be to move them out of the business, as clearly something is not quite right.

But a word of caution! We live in very litigious times. You should always get good legal advice before dismissing any member of staff and be aware that a good paperwork trail showing meetings with your employee, reasons for dismissal and the process of that dismissal will often protect you.

everything in-between!

One of the greatest challenges for many business owners is managing and motivating staff on a day to day basis. But don't despair and no need to put your head in your hands! As with everything else, you just need to take everything one step at a time.

Essential Skills

There is no harm in starting to develop now the skills you will need to deal with staff. These are some of the essential skills. Are there any of these that you need to focus on?

- ❖ good listening and questioning skills
- ❖ emotional intelligence
- ❖ cultural and diversity awareness
- ❖ assertiveness
- ❖ giving constructive feedback
- ❖ motivating and engaging staff

Dealing with problems

Should you have to deal with a staffing problem, here is one suggestion for how to approach managing it:

- ❖ Set up an initial meeting, ideally in a place where you won't be interrupted.
- ❖ To avoid your employee feeling you have ambushed them, which always starts meetings off on a bad footing, give them an hour or more to mentally prepare for your meeting.

- Be clear and concise in your communication with them.
- Encourage them to consider their situation and the impact on their work and to work with you to find a way forward.
- Set a date to meet with them again to review progress and agree any future actions.
- Make good notes of your meeting, including any actions the employee agrees to in order to turn this situation around.
- Within no more than one week of your meeting, confirm in writing your reasons for having met with your employee plus any outcomes/actions that resulted from your meeting
- Diarise your next meeting date to ensure you do what you have said you will do in respect of reviewing performance.

Processes and procedures

Managing staff is always so much easier if you have good staff management processes and procedures in place. These are the typical things that professional businesses have in place: contracts of employment; a handbook containing comprehensive policies and procedures (including absence, performance management, maternity, employee grievances, dismissal); on-boarding documentation (to help induct new staff); performance review forms; holiday forms, sickness absence forms and expenses forms.

Over the years, running my HR consultancy I have found it staggering how many companies do not have good processes and procedures for managing staff. This inevitably means that managing problems often takes ten times longer than it really should. So if you are starting to employ staff, I would strongly recommend that you make life easy for yourself by putting these things in place.

Motivating and engaging staff

Motivating and engaging staff is a challenge for all of us. There are no easy answers and the key is to understand that each and everyone in my business I meet formally with my team once every six months and part of that discussion is always about what is energising and engaging them, and equally, what is not engaging or motivating them. Having a formal performance management process is important but in your business you will need to find what works for you to ensure you keep in touch with your team and understand what is motivating and demotivating them.

Sometimes I have seen staff resign from a business due to being demotivated, but their employer had no idea that they were not happy. This can happen to both men and women of course, but I read recently that research has been done into how organisational structures can demotivate women in particular. Traditional business hierarchies are similar to the hierarchies you find in the armed forces. They provide a very rigid structure, with top down decision making and a total focus on achievement of goals. Whilst this feels comfortable and right to most men, women however often struggle in this environment as it values results above all else, with little regard for participation and effort. Women instead tend to flourish in a flexible organisation, where collaboration is the norm and where they are involved fully in the decision making and regularly recognised for their efforts and hard work to help achieve team goals.

Given the majority of workplaces contain both women and men, you will need to decide what is the most appropriate organisational structure for your business once you start employing staff.

When you are busy running your business, sometimes it's really easy not to take the time out to talk and listen to employees and therefore to understand how motivated they are at any one time. It is even harder if your business is spread across a number of locations or if you have home or remote workers.

But if you have doubts about an individual, here is just a mini-guide to checking how high their motivation levels are:

- ❖ A smart/well groomed appearance.
- ❖ A ready smile.
- ❖ A desire to take on delegated tasks and tasks that others are unable to do.
- ❖ Not clock–watching: in earlier, a shorter lunch, staying later.
- ❖ Plenty of input and contribution at team meetings.
- ❖ Walks through office/working areas with head held high actively seeking contact with other people.
- ❖ Keen for their next performance review meeting to take place.

- Demonstrates enthusiasm for work in general.
- Work is completed early or on time.
- Uses positive (rather than negative) words about workload and work organisation.
- Very good at supporting new starters.
- Good at communicating their feelings at work in a non-aggressive and easy manner.
- They ooze energy and ignore any emotional vampires around them!

monday, monday!

A couple of years ago I read about a survey conducted by Marmite that found:

Most of us find the start of the week so demoralising that we can't even bear to crack a smile until 11.16 am.

Half of us will be late for work on Monday after struggling to get up after the weekend.

As we struggle to shake off the Monday blues we will only manage three and a half hours of productive work.

45 to 54 year-olds are likely to suffer the most and will moan for around twelve minutes.

innovating in business

Are you innovative? Do you continually look to develop new ideas and opportunities?

I deliver some training for businesses wanting to encourage their staff to be more innovative. Often staff will say that they can't innovate, but I find that it's usually more a matter of creating the right environment for people to innovate in, giving them a few techniques and building their confidence in their own creativity. I come across very few people who cannot be creative or innovative when shown how to begin and what fun it can be.

You might think you don't need to innovate much now that you have your business idea and are starting to sell it. Surely innovation won't be needed for another few years? Think again! Innovation should be happening all the time in your business. Also, finding new ways of doing things internally is just as important as innovating with the products or services you sell. Our world is spinning ever faster as a result of technology, science and endless research and learning and along with it, your customers will be continually expecting more, or different, from you. You should therefore aim to be innovating from day one.

But just to get you thinking about innovation a little, I thought you might like to take a look at these quotes taken from the history books:

Everything that can be invented has been invented.
(Charles H. Duell, Director of US Patent Office 1899)

Sensible and responsible women do not want to vote.
(Grover Cleveland, 1905)

Who the hell wants to hear actors talk?
(Harry M. Warner, Warner Bros Pictures, 1927)

There is no likelihood man can ever tap the power of the atom.
(Robert Millikan, Nobel Prize in Physics, 1923)

Heavier than air flying machines are impossible.
(Lord Kelvin, President, Royal Society, 1895)

The horse is here today, but the automobile is only a novelty – a fad.
(President of Michigan Savings Bank advising against investing in the Ford Motor Company)

Video won't be able to hold on to any market it captures after the first six months. People will soon get tired of staring at a plywood box every night.
(Daryl F. Zanuck, 20th Century Fox, commenting on television in 1946)

What use could the company make of an electric toy?
(Western Union, when it turned down rights to the telephone in 1878)

Just imagine what a different world we would be living in if we had all stopped innovating and inventing just because people couldn't visualise a different way! I am sure that if you need help with innovating in business that there will be people who can support you, but this is just a short extract from my training course on innovation. I hope it provides some food for thought:

"When all think alike, then no one is thinking." Walter Lippmann
Who are the natural 'out of the box' thinkers in your business?

"We're doing the same thing over and over, with the same unsatisfactory results, yet no one ever questions what we should now do differently" Anon.
What happens in your business that really should have been reviewed/changed years ago?

"It isn't the incompetent who destroy an organization. The incompetent never get in a position to destroy it. It is those who achieved something and want to rest upon their achievements who are forever clogging things up."
F. M. Young
To what degree do people in your industry resist or not encourage change? In the long term what might this mean for your business?

"The best way to have a good idea is to have a lot of ideas."
Dr. Linus Pauling
Why do people at work so often shoot down other people's ideas?

"Innovation— any new idea—by definition will not be accepted at first. It takes repeated attempts, endless demonstrations, monotonous rehearsals before innovation can be accepted and internalized by an organization. This requires courageous patience." Warren Bennis

As well as courage and patience, what skills and attitudes are required for successful innovation?

"Creative thinking is not a talent, it is a skill that can be learnt. It empowers people by adding strength to their natural abilities which improves teamwork, productivity and where appropriate profits." Edward de Bono

Do you genuinely believe that creativity can be learnt? What stops you from becoming more creative in the way you work?

So before I finish this section, I wanted to ask you a few questions:

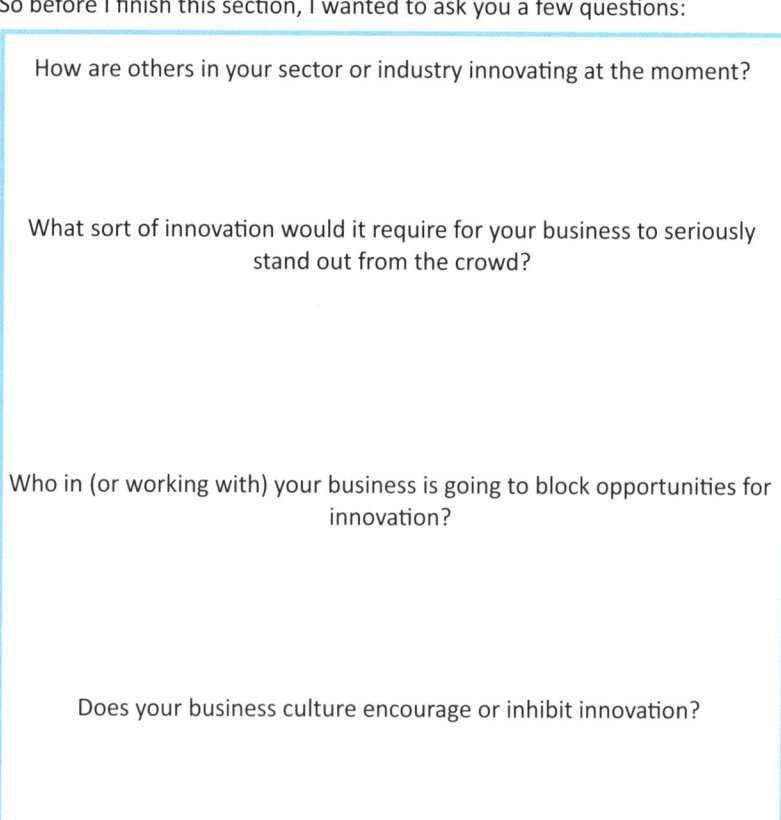

> How are others in your sector or industry innovating at the moment?
>
> What sort of innovation would it require for your business to seriously stand out from the crowd?
>
> Who in (or working with) your business is going to block opportunities for innovation?
>
> Does your business culture encourage or inhibit innovation?

business vampires

In business you have to be aware of the 'vampires'. (If you don't like the term vampire, then find another word that works for you e.g. leech) Vampires can wreck everything if you allow them to, or if you're not looking out for them. Personally, I have fallen victim to all of these vampires at certain times. But let me explain a bit more.

There are essentially four types of vampire lurking in the shadows and waiting to cause damage to either you or your business:

- Energy vampires
- Profit vampires
- Confidence vampires
- Time vampires

energy vampires

Have you ever leapt out of bed in the morning, flown into work all bright and breezy then, just ten minutes later, you are feeling flat as a pancake? What happened? Well, on arrival you asked one of your team how they were and, in response, they took the opportunity to tell you all their woes, about everything that hasn't gone right for them since the start of time, about their illnesses, their family traumas and how the world would stop turning if it wasn't for them!

So from bright and breezy you suddenly end up feeling flat and down. The energy vampires suck all your positive energy out, but when you are setting up in business you need every ounce of energy you can get.

> I laugh about it now but I once had a member of staff who arrived at work one day and told us she had stubbed her toe that morning. She then complained every time she stood up, walked, moved and quite possibly, every time she breathed.
> All day long all we heard was about her injured big toe!
> Misery from the beginning to the end of the day; and it depressed absolutely everyone! But more than depressing everyone, if you have a team drained of positive energy, the impact on your clients can be huge, as well as the impact on employee morale. So who in your family or inner group of friends is your energy vampire and what are you going to do about them to ensure they don't drain your energy?

I once read a great book called *Fish*. I have mentioned it in an earlier chapter. I expect many of you will have come across it already. I am sure it had lots of other good stuff in it, but my enduring memory of that book is about Choosing Your Attitude.

As every person, including you and me, arrives at work, we have a choice. And that choice is to choose our attitude. We can choose to be down or we can choose to be up. We can choose to find fault with everything or we can choose to always look for the positives. We can choose to work within the team or we can choose to isolate ourselves from the team. We can choose to pick ourselves up after something doesn't quite work out right or we can choose to play victim. We can choose to moan about work and life or we can choose to take time to lift all those around us.

It's odd though how some people aren't aware that they have a choice. But they do. And the choice that they make about their attitude as they walk through the door will impact throughout the day on everyone around them, on the work they do, on their own job satisfaction and on the clients or customers they meet.

What choice about attitude did you take into work or life with you yesterday?

If you had made a different choice could your day have turned out differently?

It's not always easy, but here are a few tips for remaining positive on even a bad day:

Find a mirror and smile at yourself. And keep smiling until it becomes less forced and starts to feel more comfortable. Then grin at yourself. Then chuckle as you remind yourself of everything that is going well in your life and work.

Remove yourself from the vicinity of people who will add to your low mood. Stay away from them all day.

Go and be near people who you know will always raise your spirits and keep you buoyant.

Go online and take a look at a few motivational quotes. Some of them might remind you of the bigger picture or how things are often not as bad as we think they are.

Stop dwelling on what you didn't do right and instead jot down at least ten things that you really are great at. No false modesty allowed!

Choose tasks that will work to your strengths today rather than those you find hard.

Go and do some exercise and focus on your body rather than what's going on in your head.

Be disciplined enough to do the task you really don't want to do, but that ultimately is what is putting you in your bad mood.

Find a few easy wins for your day. Ticking things off our list always makes us feel good.

Aside from *Fish*. Another good book that I know many have read is called Feel the Fear But Do It Anyway. Often fear makes people withdrawn and negative in their attitude. It can be fear of anything in business, including fear of rejection, fear of failure, fear of making a mistake, fear of letting others down etc. If you are fearful or if you know people who are and know that this impacts on their positive energy at work, then why not suggest they take a look at this book.

Sometimes, though, we might choose a positive attitude at work, but are then surrounded by people who do not have a positive attitude and who clearly have no inclination to change their attitude; what then?

My view is that when you are setting up a business you need as much positive energy around you as possible. Energy vampires can do enormous damage in the early days if you allow them to.
My suggestion therefore is that you spend as little time as possible with people who drag you down. You get rid of suppliers who sap your energy and replace them with suppliers who bring in energy. You get rid of staff or associates who sap your energy and you avoid those places where you know the negative people are likely to meet to moan (water coolers, workplace kitchens, coffee shops etc.).

But it's a bit harder to distance yourself from customers or clients who sap your energy. So a few tips:

- Always greet them with a smile on your face.
- Try to avoid asking them how they are. Ask another polite question or make another polite statement instead that will provide no opportunity for them to moan.
- Avoid small talk as this can lead to the moans and groans.
- Be prepared for your meetings or be efficient in the way you deal with them to allow little time for either extra talk or the moans and groans to creep in.
- Always have an excuse ready so you can excuse yourself as quickly as possible.
- Gently chide them about their negativity and ask them about what is going well for them – e.g. 'Oh what a shame to hear that, but tell me

Some people choose to engage with everyone they meet all day and pass on their own positive energy to those who aren't so positive. This is absolutely wonderful that people do this, but if this is you, be very careful of getting worn out with the effort. Do what feels natural, but never feel it is your duty to persuade everyone to see what is good with the world!

profit vampires

In my business, every two weeks we email an HR Blast to our clients. Below I've reproduced one that we sent out a few months ago about profit vampires. In this Blast we refer to employees who could be profit vampires, but almost all of these points could also relate to you, the business owner! Have a read and see what you think. If you would like to sign up to our HR Blasts, sign up by scanning the QR code below.

* scan me

As a business, we often talk at Jaluch about the vampires at work. Today we turn to your organisation's profit vampires:

Profit vampire #1
Petty pilferers

It's only a calculator, it's only a stapler, it's only a few pens, it's only one Post-It note block ... Whilst this appears to be less of a problem than it has been in the past, stationery cupboard vampires acquire your property and take it home with them. The problem is that if everyone does this then it can really add up.

Profit vampire #2
Expenses embezzlers

This vampire is great at adding a little here, there and everywhere to their expenses claim. Sometimes they go a 'little' wild and add in

Profit vampire #3
Commercial catastrophes

This vampire is a manager. The manager who agrees overtime without thinking whether work could be better organised during normal hours, or the manager who agrees for two people to make a business trip when just one is actually sufficient, or the manager who agrees a pay rise without doing the sums first. They might be a great manager, doing most of their job well, but their failure to see the bigger commercial picture might be costing you dear.

Profit vampire #4
Property pirates

Even though your company policy says that staff will be disciplined if they are careless with company property, companies seldom manage in this way, therefore vampire #4 is the employee who endlessly damages or loses company property. From the company vehicle and laptop to the phone, shredder or even workstation, have you ever added up how much certain notorious staff cost you in endless damage? They don't do it deliberately, but they don't particularly take care of your property either.

Profit vampire #5
Sickie swindlers

Those employees who just want a few duvet days or extra rest days after strenuous weekends. How much would it cost you if each member of staff in your business took two sickies a year?

Profit vampire #6
Serial slackers

This is the vampire that causes wastage as a result of work having to be repeated due to carelessness first time around. Or clients who are lost due to customer care calls not taking place, or even the cost of responding to complaints if staff handle your customers badly due to a 'can't be bothered' attitude.

Profit vampire #7
Responsibility wrigglers

This is the profit vampire that causes wastage and loss as a result of turning a blind eye to something that they don't think is their responsibility.

Perhaps the dripping tap, the colleague who's fiddling their expenses, not turning the lights off when no one is 'home', or perhaps not telling their manager that Petra spends most days twiddling her thumbs due to lack of work.

Profit vampire #8
Freebie fritterers

This is the oh-so-generous vampire who can't resist offering your customer just a little discount on this and that or a fee reduction because they like them, or who throws in a few extra freebies just to keep them on-side. All these add-ons and discounts cost you serious amounts of money over the course of a year.

Profit vampire #9
Hapless hesitators

This is the profit vampire who fails to manage his or her probationers, always wanting to give them one more chance, or find ways to give them the benefit of the doubt rather than take action and dismiss them. The same happens with those who have passed probation, but whose managers hesitate to discipline them and remove them from the business, if that is what is needed, just because it's easier than having a confrontation or holding a tough meeting.

Profit vampire #10
Short-term winners (long-term sinners)

These are the vampires who push their luck with clients. They have a tendency to oversell, overbill or overprice things, and whilst they might get you this sale, they probably won't get you the next sale due to not building solid relationships with clients, and they might even have lost you the customer for good.

In my experience, before you employ any (or many) staff, and before you have a few years' business experience under your belt, the real profit vampire in the organisation could be you. Take another look at vampires 3, 8 and 10 to see if these could ever apply to you. Number 8 in particular is, I think, a real danger zone for many new businesses – and I am not preaching here; I have made as many mistakes in business as you are going to make!

'Let's be honest. There's not a business anywhere that is without problems. Business is complicated and imperfect. Every business everywhere is staffed with imperfect human beings and exists by providing a product or service to other imperfect human beings'

(Bob Parsons)

confidence vampires

In this section I want to say a few words about maternity leave, Queen Bees, mums at the school gate, expectations and our irritating inner voice.

Recently I went to a gathering where all the women there were in their mid to late forties. I expected to hear about their careers and successes to date, but apart from a few, most were not working or, if they were, it was in roles that appeared to be well below their capabilities given that almost every single one of them had a degree of one sort or another. Overwhelmingly, I felt that they were not happy with what they were doing, but that they lacked the confidence to either return to work following a long period of being at home whilst raising children or to change their career to something that would bring them satisfaction.

This is something that is really critical to address, as low self-esteem and low levels of confidence can hold women back enormously from realising their dreams.

In life you will know that some people were born oozing self-confidence whilst others are born with very little and have to develop it over time. There are also, of course, plenty in between who are relatively confident in life.

But the older I have got, the more I have also encountered those who once were confident, but who have lost that initial confidence after receiving a few of life's knocks or being away from work for too long. Confidence loss, though, does not just apply to women in the workplace, as I have seen it happen to both men and women.

One of the most common reasons for confidence loss amongst women is, I believe, absence from work. Another common reason is having spent too much time in a role surrounded by confidence vampires – people who continually tell you that you are not good enough or that you don't fit in. But first let's look at the absence from work issue.

> HSE 2010 (UK) report on absence and job loss
> At the point at which employees reach their sixth week of absence, almost one in five people will stay off sick and eventually leave work.

Research has shown that anyone who is off sick from work for longer than a few months begins to lose their confidence, and the expectation is generally that if someone has been off for over three months it will become increasingly hard to ever get them to return to work. It is therefore not surprising that women often face severe confidence issues if they have been off work as a result of having a baby (or babies!).

I know that in some areas of the world women only get a few weeks' maternity leave and so return to work very quickly after having a baby. (Or they don't return at all!) However, in other countries maternity leave provision has been increasing dramatically over the past decade or so. I am sure the women in those countries with shorter periods of maternity leave will wonder how great it might be to have a longer period of leave; however, keeping the maternity leave period short does in fact mean that women are not off work for so long that they lose their confidence in their ability to add value at work.

It's an interesting dilemma and one which never seems to be discussed at all: Do you want to spend longer off work with your young family or do you want to retain your self-confidence?

> Here are a few examples of current maternity leave provision around the world:
>
> Netherlands – 16 weeks on full pay with 4-6 weeks having to be taken before the birth
>
> Sweden – 480 days of leave per child (can be split equally between both parents) of which 420 of these days are paid at a rate of 80% of your salary up to a defined upper limit.
>
> UAE – 45 days on full pay
>
> UK – 12 months leave with 90% of salary in the first 6 weeks and then a weekly maternity allowance up to the end of the first 9 month period.

One of the problems of course is that women going off on maternity leave will always choose to believe that 'confidence loss' will not happen to them. It must seem unimaginable to a woman that you can work for five or ten years, but then could lose your confidence after just six weeks of absence. The evidence that this is the case though is compelling and consistent. Maternity leave is therefore one of the greatest 'confidence vampires' you need to be aware of.

Maternity leave aside, women also lack confidence generally in comparison to their male colleagues. A lifetime of having the media, other businesses, friends and sometimes even our families suggesting that women do not have what it takes to succeed in business is enormously damaging to women's confidence. Just last year in the UK a survey of male directors from the UK's top firms found that 12% of the male directors believed that having more women on boards of directors would not just have a neutral impact on business, but a detrimental one, despite evidence suggesting that diverse boards are not only more profitable, but grow faster as well. When I tweeted about the 12% of men who said that we women have no value, a number of men sent me messages that all essentially said the same thing: it is not 12% at all; to get a true reflection of what men feel about women in business, you need to at least double it to 24%!

This research clearly relates to the UK but no doubt you will have a sense of the different attitudes to women in business in different countries of the world.

But be under no illusions, it is not just men who do not believe that women have what it takes to contribute at the highest levels in business; other women too can undermine confidence enormously. There have been books written on the subject and I will leave you to go and read those if this topic interests you (you might start with The Twisted Sisterhood by Kelly Valen). Successful women who have made it up the career ladder also have a tendency to kick out the ladder from beneath them (thanks to Professor David Clutterbuck for his thoughts on this) as they like to retain their 'Queen Bee' status of being among the few to have made it. At the opposite end of the scale those mums at the school gate who like to suggest that working mothers are neglecting their children are equally damaging, if not more so, as not only do they not support us or encourage us, but they often go out of their way to criticise and undermine us by hitting our confidence where it hurts the most – whether we are good mothers or not!

You have to develop a bit of a thick skin in business though and women should NEVER beat themselves up about their lack of confidence in business. I see many women doing this and feeling that they continually have to justify themselves or prove themselves better than men or find businesses that don't compete with men. But this isn't necessary. You might have lost your confidence or you might generally lack confidence, but actually setting up and running your own business is a simply fantastic way to build your confidence and create a working environment that suits you. You will also not have to continually justify your right to be in work or explain why you choose to operate differently to your competitor down the street. You can be you!

I don't want to dwell on it too much, but another confidence vampire is 'expectation'. This links back to my chapter on ambition. What are the expectations of your family, friends, neighbours, university lecturers? Do they expect much of you? Do they expect enough of you? Do they think that whilst you might have it in you to set up a hobby business, you don't have what it takes to develop it into something really successful? Do they think that you should focus more on family than on work? Do they think that women just 'dabble' in the men's world of business?

Do they think that women who make it to the top only do so because legislation rather than hard work has got them there? Do they think you are on a par with some of the well-known and successful business people in your local community? Do they humour you, rather than encourage you? You might not like the question, but what I would like you to ask yourself is: 'Who would like to see me fail?' or if you prefer it, 'Who really wouldn't be bothered if I did fail?' Now make sure you distance yourself from those people. No business person needs people near them who get their kicks out of other people's failures rather than their success.

Now, can I ask you to think about something: of all the voices around you, which is the loudest? I really hope it is attached to someone who has the highest, rather than the lowest, expectations of you.

One woman who knows that many around her would smile if she failed is Katie Price. As a model in her earlier years, Katie was known as Jordan. It doesn't matter whether you have heard of her or not, but Katie is mercilessly criticised in the media but seldom, if ever, recognised for her commercial nous and absolute determination. The last time I checked, a report suggested her net worth was around £45 million. This figure may or may not be true but she is very wealthy and she has countless businesses to her name. But people only tend to see her make-up, her clothes, her relationships and her lack of formal education (she left school at sixteen). Many entrepreneurs are doing what they do to prove themselves to their families, friends or societies, although few admit that openly. But here is Katie's quote:

> 'I'm very ambitious, and success is the best revenge on everyone who said, "you can't do this, you won't do this".'

Moving away from the impact of expectations though, another confidence vampire is of course our inner voice! That little voice that asks us whether we really have what it takes to set up and run this business. That asks whether we know what we are doing, that suggests we might fail, that makes us doubt ourselves and that endlessly makes us feel guilty about neglecting our family, house or husband/partner. The little voice in our heads has a lot to answer for!

I once had a business coach who told me that over the years he had not yet come across a male business owner who didn't have a little inner voice that also suggested he might not have what it takes, or he might fail or he might be found out as someone who doesn't know all that people think he knows. So go easy on your inner voice and know that whilst men seldom talk about it, they have one too!

One of the most exasperating things about women is our ability to talk ourselves into a downward spiral about why we can't achieve or do it, or shouldn't be able to achieve it, or really won't achieve it… Utter nonsense – we just have to know that that is what we tend to do and then make sure we don't allow ourselves the luxury of doing it!

I know it is really tough to do, which is why you need to surround yourself with supportive and encouraging people who have the right expectations of you. I talked about this in the very early chapters of this book and I don't apologise for repeating it here as it is crucial that you ensure that the people around you will support you and give you confidence. So know who those people are and keep them close.

> It took me fifteen years of being in business before I gave myself a serious talking-to and took the steps I needed to take to begin to really improve my own confidence levels. That's a lot of wasted time so if this is an issue for you, I suggest you tackle it right from the start – then you will be well ahead of me!

time vampires

And last but not least, we have the time vampires that can have such a huge impact on us and our businesses.

If you run out of time ...

- ❖ You may end up working through the night (yes, I have been there many, many times!).
- ❖ You produce work or products that are not up to scratch (yes, I have done that at times – although not too often I hope!).
- ❖ You spend so much time fulfilling orders or delivering your service that you run out of time to spend on seeking new business (this can be catastrophic for a young business and yes, I have made this mistake too!).
- ❖ You mess up your health as you skip exercise and meals due to being too busy trying to catch up (yes, I've done this one too!).
- ❖ It forces you to be so heads-down when you are trying to keep up with tasks that you can damage your whole business by not seeing the bigger picture (and yes, I've been guilty of this one too!).

I do remember as a child thinking that the school holidays were endlessly long and that time went by so slowly, but those thoughts are long gone. For years now, I have never had enough time in the day to do what I want to do, and it is my weekly prayer that someone grants me forty-eight hours in every day. I can't think of the last time I ever got bored; it must have been decades ago.

And running a business just means that you have even less time than everyone else. There must surely be a law of science or mathematical equation that relates to business ownership versus time available. If you can come up with the equation I would love to see it!

So you need to be careful with your time.

Here is a summary of the eight time vampires that I see many female business owners not dealing with either often enough or early enough – it may be that just one or two of these apply to you, but knowing where your time might get wasted is important.

Time vampire #1
Perfection

Many women I know have a tendency to always seek perfection in what they are doing. In business, however, you seldom have this luxury and you must produce work to a standard that is 'fit for purpose', rather than perfect. Perfection is often not an option if you wish to make any money and keep your sanity.

If you know that you have a tendency towards perfectionism, then I strongly recommend you take some time to think through how you are going to manage this in your business. You will need to learn where the opportunities are for compromise in respect of perfection and where it is okay to continue to look for perfection. You must learn to compromise if you are to survive.

Time vampire #2
Networking

When many women set up in business they have no pre-existing network of business contacts. This is a fundamental difference between men and women when starting out in business. Even throughout their early life in education, men are continually meeting people and either including them in their little black book of useful contacts or wiping the memory of ever having met them. In contrast, women meet people throughout their life and tend to decide whether those people are in or out of the pool of people they want to be friends with.

At the point at which they start up in business, therefore, men have useful contacts and women have friends. So women often need to start their networking from scratch and this can take a long time.

An added complication is that women tend to seek to create a relationship before ever talking about the serious stuff of business, whereas men, within minutes of meeting you, seek to elicit information about potential mutual business. In a quick-moving networking environment, therefore, the women haven't even started to talk about business before the networking function ends! I am exaggerating of course, but in essence men are great at networking and women still have a lot to learn about it.

As a result of this, women often attend far too many networking events as they play catch-up in creating business contacts, and the time they spend at those networking events is not always well spent in terms of creating sales opportunities – too much chat! Its not often I suggest that women should seek to mimic the approach of men, but in respect of networking, I think that learning from the men could be very useful if you don't want this to be one of your time vampires.

Time vampire #3
Customer care

It won't come as a great surprise to many of you to learn that women tend to focus more on the customer-care side of life than many men. It is probably in the nature of many of us to want to be liked by our customers and to want to ensure that they have got what they need. It's not just a female trait, though, as some great companies like Apple really pride themselves on their customer service, but I suspect this is more of a strategic decision than just a desire to be liked and to serve!

It is no bad thing, of course, to deliver great service and be held accountable for that by your customers, but you need to be careful not to allow customer care to become one of your business's time vampires. By all means deliver a service, but remember that you have money to make too.

Time vampire #4
Doing the tasks you really should outsource

Have you ever spent five hours doing something and at the end of it you look at what you have done and say to yourself, 'I really should have paid someone to do that for me as they could have cracked it in an hour'? Some business owners are great at false economies, but doing a job yourself when you really should outsource or delegate it can be a massive time vampire.

So what jobs do you huff and puff over? Sorting out your technology, end-of-month finances, creating a website, trying to work out how to get your website up the search engines, writing an article for some PR? These are all the tasks that I have seen people sweating over and the end result is often not spectacular, even though days of effort have gone into it. If this rings bells with you, learn what you need to outsource before you waste your time doing something you really shouldn't be doing. It's a false economy.

Time vampire #5
Interfering/micromanagement

In a similar vein, enormous amounts of time can be wasted if you spend your life interfering with work that you have delegated or outsourced to others. By all means set the required standard, but at the point at which you know you are interfering or controlling, you need to step back if your own management style is not to become an enormous time vampire.

As part of the business I run we produce employment documentation for clients. This includes contracts of employment and employment policies which we incorporate into an employment handbook. In seventeen or more years of trading we must have done thousands of these. The normal process is that we take a brief, create the documents, return to the client and then spend an hour or so talking about the documents and making small amendments or additions here and there.

I recall one client, many years ago. The meeting to discuss the employee handbook took nearly two days. I was there for seven hours during the first session and then six hours a week later. We went through every word in that document, discussing the grammar, the spelling, the sentence construction, the law, the options – although amazingly we never discussed the paper it was printed on! It was of course the client's right to work through those documents and as a business we charge for each hour we work for the client so it was good money for us, but it is just not possible to micromanage work like this in today's environment when we all have so much else to do. If you are outsourcing work to an expert, by all means keep on eye on what they are doing, but be very careful to understand where the line is drawn between good management and micro management as this can be a great time vampire.

Time vampire #6
Lack of focus

A lovely guy I met once in the Middle East said he was a global sales director for his firm. He said that he spent most of his time in the Gulf and some in India. I asked him when he was last in the States. He said he hadn't been there at all whilst doing this particular role. I asked him how was it possible for him to be a global sales director but to only cover certain countries. His answer was that in business you can flail around and hope that something will work or otherwise you can be really picky about where and when you are going to do business in full knowledge that focus will bring better rewards. He said his strategy was to do the research, identify the best potential markets to sell into and then spend time in those markets. He added that the job title was just paperwork, the sales he made ensured business success and that too many of us often get caught up in the 'paperwork' stuff rather than focusing on what is really important: generating revenue.

Are you flailing around trying to find a sale someplace or have you sat down and worked out your focus for where your attention and time is going to be?

If you have attended four networking events in recent months, with hindsight, could you identify which ones of those were likely to result in your meeting the right people or having the right conversations? Equally with hindsight can you identify those ones that you really should have known would not be a great use of your time?

And in terms of what you sell, can you identify what products or services absorb your time but generate little revenue, versus those products or services that absorb time but generate good revenue? Don't let your lack of focus become a time vampire!

Over the past year I cannot even begin to count the number of women I have met who tell me that they have three, four or even five jobs/businesses. They are proud as punch as they tell me about selling on cookware, make-up, clothing, or giving massages or beauty treatments, or running around selling helium balloons for children's parties. None of their businesses ever seem interconnected.

Often I ask which of their 'jobs' they like the most. They look at me bemused and say they like all of them. I might be wrong, but I am almost always left with the distinct impression that is not true. I do believe that many of these women are taking on more and more opportunities to become part of a distribution network (often for some American giant) or selling services or products in the belief that if they have enough fingers in enough pies, they will earn a living and they will be able to hold their heads up to their partners and families and say 'I do pay my way and I do contribute to the household.'

But is this a good way to do business? Is this a focused way to do business? If I could hazard a guess I would say that not one of these women has a business plan in place and not one has sales targets attached to each endeavour. So how do they know how much energy or time to put into each endeavour? How do they know when its time to pull out of one endeavour as it's preventing the success of another? I just hope that some of these women don't look back in ten years' time and question how they have been spending their time and what financial return they have had for their efforts.

There is a great expression that might apply here: 'It's great to be busy, unless you are just busy being busy.'

Time vampire #7
Doing but not thinking

A common feature of many of us is that we spend so much time doing, we are left with insufficient time for thinking. But not thinking – and planning – can then result in us wasting time doing the wrong things. I once met a man on a plane who said he had endless backache, he didn't sleep well and he was permanently stressed. He said his boss frequently told him that he needed to 'get off the dance floor and onto the balcony' if he was ever to make his job easier. He told me that his response to his boss always was 'I don't have time'. I won't even go into who was the greater liability in that business; the manager who didn't take the necessary steps to change things or the boss who allowed him to make stupid excuses about why he couldn't do what both of them agreed was really important.

It's a cycle, isn't it, because if you don't force yourself to take time out to think, then you will never see what it is you need to see to enable you to change things or do things differently. Failure to think it though is as much a time vampire as any of the other time vampires I have mentioned. So make some space or time for yourself to think. I have time to think as nowadays I swim most days of the week right at the start of the day and my swimming time is always my thinking and planning time. What thinking time can you introduce into your day to ensure you get to really think about stuff each and every day?

Time vampire #8
Poor personal organisation

And last but not least, a time vampire that impacts many of us is our poor personal organisation. If we are badly organised then the impact of that can be widespread in our business. In terms of time it means that often we have to do work ourselves because we have run out of time to delegate it to someone else, or we have to work through the night because we didn't take time out to plan how to resource the project properly, or we turn up at the wrong venue for a meeting as a result of having failed to check the details, or we rush out of the office or shop and leave behind essential documents, which means that we have to have two meetings with our insurance broker rather than just one. And the list goes on. The impact of poor personal organisation is enormous and a time vampire you might do well to try to keep under control!

Identify here three things you could do to improve your personal organisation as your life gets busier and busier setting up and running your business:

CHAPTER EIGHT

sales

The lifeblood of any business you set up is going to be the sales you make.

You need to think about how you are going to make your sales, how you are going to let the market know that you exist so they come to you to buy, how you are going to compete against others in the market, how you are going to ensure that customers come back to you time after time to buy, and how you are going to deliver the goods/service once the sale has been made. There are, of course, hundreds of other considerations, but I hope that the few I have included will get you thinking.

If you want to spend some time on this area then I suggest you buy a specialist book that just focuses on sales skills or sales psychology. One book that a few people have found useful is called Sales Dogs by Blair Singer, but look around as there are hundreds on the market.

Until such time as you have bought your book on sales, here are a few of my views and observations from my time in business.

your elevator pitch

If you have never heard of an elevator pitch before, let me explain. The idea is that if you are in elevator and someone asks you what you do, you will have just the time it takes for the elevator to reach its floor to summarise your business in a way that will interest or intrigue them enough to want to meet or talk with you again.

An elevator pitch is therefore a short speech of just a few sentences that describes or promotes your business. Can you summarise what you do or sell in just three or four short sentences? Give it a go!

It's important that you create an elevator pitch because, more times that you can count, you will be asked to describe what you do or sell when out networking, meeting clients for the first time, talking to suppliers etc. If you don't yet have one, you ought to develop one before you attend your next networking event.

Here is an example of an elevator pitch that could be used for my business:

Jaluch is an HR and training consultancy that supports hundreds of employers with their staffing issues and employment law problems. We also support organisations by developing and training their line managers in people management skills. Our differentiator in the market is that we always seek to be commercial and pragmatic in our approach to managing staff. In delivering training solutions we have a reputation for being innovative and creative.

A few tips in creating your elevator pitch:

- ❖ Keep it simple and avoid jargon.
- ❖ Use words that assume the person you are talking to is not in your profession or industry.
- ❖ Include one or two of your differentiators or USPs (unique selling points).
- ❖ If you want to, and if it is relevant information to those you talk to, also include your corporate values.
- ❖ Be prepared to change your elevator pitch at a moment's notice to reflect the interests of the person you are speaking to.

NOTES

you can start drafting out your elevator pitch here

what sort of salesperson are you?

It might be that as a business owner you do not see yourself as a salesperson. But the reality is that as a business owner you need to be a salesperson. When I first set up my very first business I decided that I would never need to sell (as it filled me with total fear!) and if I got my marketing right then the clients would come to me.

Years down the line I can see that my strategy worked in part. The clients have come to us and I can't think of any time in the past ten years or more where we have done any cold calling. However, my strategy was never entirely successful as you really cannot get away from the need to sell.

If you are an expert in sales or feel really comfortable with it, then I suggest you skip on to the next part of this chapter. But those of you who are not so sure about the whole sales 'thing' need to read on. I wonder if I had worked out right at the start what part of the sales process I didn't like, I might have felt much more comfortable. I really also should have prioritised some formal development for myself in this area right at the start.

Along with knowing how to use spreadsheets, I would suggest that sales training is an absolutely essential skill for you to invest in if you wish to maximise your chances of success in your new venture. Be careful whom you pay to give you sales training, though, as there are lots of courses out there in the market that really are a waste of time and money.

Essentially, I see the different tasks for businesses when selling B2B (business to business) as:

the groundwork for sales

- Creating sales information (including information displayed on a website)
- Attracting enquiries to your business
- Researching/information-gathering

first steps towards a sale
- ❖ Cold calling to arrange meetings
- ❖ Warm calling to arrange meetings

sales meetings
- ❖ Attending prospect meetings
- ❖ Taking the brief
- ❖ Telling them how much it costs
- ❖ Drafting proposals

making the sale
- ❖ Following up on proposals and asking for the sale
- ❖ Closing the sale

following the sale
- ❖ Further down the line, asking for repeat business
- ❖ Asking for referrals and testimonials

In selling to B2C (business to consumer) the sales tasks are:

the groundwork for sales
- ❖ Attracting visitors to you (your shop, online site, hotel etc.)
- ❖ Inviting people in to see what you have

making the sale
- ❖ Listening to what it is they are looking for and identifying if you can provide it
- ❖ Providing an opportunity to buy (online, face to face, by phone etc.)

following the sale
- ❖ Asking for repeat business
- ❖ Asking for referrals and testimonials

How about you put a star against any of those activities you don't like or that you feel uncomfortable doing. This should help you narrow down where your difficulties with sales might lie. And please don't just put a star next to everything; really assess what you feel comfortable doing and what you feel uncomfortable doing.

From what I have seen I would suggest there are four principal reasons why many business owners worry about the sales aspect of their job:

Fear. I believe that many people get anxious if they fear they will be rejected. To me the obvious areas for rejection are cold calling, saying how much it costs and following up on proposals. To a lesser extent, given that by now you have a relationship with this client, there could be a fear factor involved in asking for repeat business and asking for referrals and testimonials.

Research. If you are someone who likes to be out and about all day then it might be that your weak area is going to be around the initial research and then the following-up.

Writing skills. This includes those aspects of sales that require writing, including sales literature, taking a brief, proposals and emails to follow up. (Did you know that around 20% of business owners have a difficulty such as dyslexia or literacy generally which inevitably impacts on confidence in this area?)

Personal organisation. What surprised me being new to sales when I set up was how there is quite disciplined process to follow with sales. You can't just do one part of it and then walk away in hope that someone else will complete the sale for you. You need to work through it step by step and ensure that you are organised enough to progress things in a timely manner.

NOTES

what is going to be your particular challenge when selling?

what are you going to do to overcome this challenge before it impacts on your sales?

It is a well-known fact that women often 'don't ask'. In the HR industry over the years I have seen numerous examples where women leave work disgruntled due to lack of progress, but readily acknowledge that they never asked for a promotion. I have also heard numerous women moaning about a lack of pay rises but also admitting that they never asked for one. Women tend to take the view that if they work hard enough their work will speak for itself and their manager will reflect that by offering a promotion or a pay rise. In reality this is living in dreamland. Promotions and pay rises are, for the most part, only given to those who repeatedly ask for them. It's just a shame no-one told the women about that!

There have also been countless times when I myself have set out what I sell, but never directly asked for the sale. I assumed that was a given. But it isn't and if you want the sale, you have to ask for it. I cannot emphasise this enough: women 'not asking' is a massive problem and holds them back enormously both in employment and self-employment. I know I have suggested this earlier on in this book, but if you want to read more on the subject, I suggest you buy Why Women Don't Ask by Linda Babcock and Sarah Laschever.

Next I want to get you to think just a little about what style of salesperson you want to be. I am not a sales guru in the slightest, but these are some of the styles I come across most often:

Formal – written briefs, agendas for meetings, written proposals, formal emails. This approach looks and feels professional although sometimes it feels a bit like using a hammer to crack a nut and can feel a bit cold when on the receiving end. I would suggest that suppliers over the years who have gone down this route have probably the weakest relationship with me. However the terms of the relationship are always clear and the exit route if ever I don't want to deal with them anymore is often set down right at the outset, which can make things easier. I am sure many business owners like this approach as the formality of the paperwork can create a sense of protection and confidence. I find that experts and specialists often tend to go for the more formal approach when selling.

Informal and friendly – often there is a distinct lack of paperwork in this sales approach but you do feel that you have talked and they have listened and now understand what you need or want. Whether they truly understand is another matter, but you feel as though they do! I like this approach personally, but it does create problems if ever there is an issue to be resolved as there is no clear way to resolve it and no clear responsibility for doing so either. Personally I do a lot of repeat sales with this kind of salesperson as I always enjoy the sales process.

Best mate – I know I am not the only one who detests salespeople who telephone and their opening words are 'Hi, how are you today?' Do they know me, do they care, do they want me to answer? No, no and no. So, if you are not my best friend, please don't act as though you are. I hate that and I know many others do too. An odd thing about this 'best mate' style is that some of us use an appointment-making service and whilst we would never use this 'best mate' style ourselves, we actually have no clue as to whether the appointment-making service we have appointed does this or not. It might be worth checking how they actually make your appointments on your behalf if you want a consistent sales style across your business.

'I won't take no for an answer' or 'I'll frighten you into saying yes' or 'You can say no as often as you like but I'm never going to listen' – this is another style I avoid. There is a fine line between assertiveness and pushiness and no-one really likes the latter when being sold to. It certainly is a lousy way to sell as pretty much all of us business owners rely on repeat sales and referrals in this day and age and the hard sell or fear factor sell never leaves a good taste in your mouth.

> a dilemma: My business works in the field of HR (as well as training, we provide day-to-day employment law and employee relations support to hundreds of organisations). A regular dilemma for us has been about how to market ourselves. Our competitors, particularly the legal firms and the large firms that sell HR support coupled with tribunal insurance, often use scare tactics to make sales. They use some recent employment tribunal outcome where a breathtaking compensation award was made to an employee and then sell their services on the back of that.

> I know that people do buy when they are scared and they wish to protect their business; however, to me, many are scared into buying products or services that they just do not need, or at a level they do not need. Oftentimes the tribunal case that has been used in the scare tactic is just not typical of other cases going through the system and there is a specific reason why the compensation is enormous.
>
> As a business we have always said that integrity is critical, therefore we will not use scare tactics to get people to buy. But in pursuing this route we lose sales to our competitors. So should we stick to your principles or should we pursue sales contrary to our principles? This might be a decision you have to make one day.

As with many aspects of business, there is no right or wrong answer as to what sales style or approach you should adopt. You will need to decide what is right for you given your personal style, your business values, the products/services you sell and the nature of the market you are selling into.

But once you have decided, here are a few things you might do:

- ❖ Check that your sales style in meetings with customers reflects the style in your literature and on your website. An inconsistent style confuses customers.
- ❖ Check that any telesales agency you use mirrors your sales style.
- ❖ Check that any employees you take on also consistently reflect your agreed business sales style.
- ❖ Think about the culture of any marketing or PR agencies you work with, ensuring that they both understand and mirror your chosen sales style. (I once worked with a PR agency who just never 'got' our more informal approach to communications and working with them was like pulling teeth.)

offering incentives

Bogof (buy one get one free), two for one, three for the price of two, 10% off, £100 off, buy this and we'll throw in x for free, buy now and get an early bird discount, free postage and packing ...

Some of the most challenging debates we have had over the years in my business are about incentives. There are times when sales are flagging, when you are introducing new products, when you have cash flow problems, when you are in the middle of a predictably slow month (e.g. December in the UK or Ramadan in the Middle East) and inevitably the discussion turns to whether it would be sensible to offer customers incentives.

I think the debates in my business over the years have demonstrated that there is no easy answer to this one. If you discount too often you might undervalue what you sell. If you discount too much you can damage your profit margin, so whilst this might help cash flow in the short term, it could in the long term damage your business. And if you never discount, your customers might think that they can get a better bargain by going elsewhere!

Just one small word of advice: just because others are discounting does not mean that you have to. Always take your time to think through what you are trying to achieve and what level of discount, if any, is right for your business.

negotiating

If you are a confident negotiator, skip to the next section. If you are not such a confident negotiator, here are a few of my thoughts ...

It has been my observation when volunteering in schools over the years that girls in the UK lack confidence with negotiation, whereas all the boys feel very confident that they can negotiate well. Whether the boys actually can negotiate or not may well be a different matter! I don't know if this is a cultural thing within the UK or whether the same applies in other countries. I suspect it will apply in some but not in others.

And if this is my experience with a difference between boys and girls, then it goes without saying that the difference in respect of confidence in negotiating will still exist between men and women. I do know some women who are great negotiators, but I know many who hesitate to negotiate or who will not negotiate at all.

When I have asked about this lack of confidence around negotiation, these are some of the reasons I have been given:

- ❖ My father thinks that boys should always negotiate but that it is not 'seemly' for girls to negotiate. (I explored this with them and understood that the fathers were suggesting that negotiation is an aggressive behaviour and therefore not suitable for girls and women.)
- ❖ I don't want to appear aggressive.
- ❖ I don't like confrontation.
- ❖ I fear conflict.
- ❖ I don't know how to negotiate; I don't know what the process is.
- ❖ I don't want to insult them or ruin the deal before we even begin by suggesting a price that is too low (or high), but I don't know what would be considered too low (high) as a starting point.
- ❖ I expect them to offer me a fair price in the first instance.
- ❖ I think boys will always be good at negotiation but it's not what girls do.

I don't know which of these you agree or disagree with and, at the end of the day, they are all different people's perceptions (although the first bullet was discussed and agreed with around thirty girls of various ethnicities in one session) but perhaps some of this might get you thinking a little about why you hesitate to negotiate.

What is interesting of course is that professional negotiators would disagree that negotiation is an aggressive or confrontational act if done properly. Good negotiation should aim for a win/win outcome rather than a win/lose outcome which would be the case if one party were seeking to dominate the other. But if the perception of many is that it is confrontational and potentially aggressive then that perception is what will drive people's behaviours around negotiation.

It took me over twelve years of being in business before I paid to go on a negotiation skills course. I cannot begin to imagine how much money over the years I might have saved (or made) had I gone on that course twelve years earlier.

What was interesting also was that as a result of going on the course, I became more aware of negotiation which, in turn, had a knock on effect to my staff who also started to negotiate more despite not having been on the course themselves!

a story to make you smile ...

My daughter has many strengths, but she was not born a natural negotiator, but interestingly, in her first ever major purchase at the age of seventeen, she landed herself a great deal.

Having just passed her driving test she phoned her insurance company to inform them she had passed and to get a quote for full car insurance. The woman quoted her £2900. In shock (although this is in fact a typical price for insurance for someone her age) and not having a clue what to say in response, my daughter went quiet. Presumably misinterpreting the silence, the woman in the call centre then offered her £2200. Again my daughter was silent but this time she told me she was rapidly trying to think how much the credit limit on her card was and panicking about whether she would be allowed to pay it in two instalments if £2200 was over her credit limit. Given the continuing silence, the insurance lady then came back and offered her £1700. Having found her voice, my daughter then said 'okay'.

Listening in to her call, I couldn't decide whether I should be impressed or stunned at what a fantastic deal she had just landed herself!

Two interesting lessons though:
1. How valuable it can be to just shut up and wait for the other party to speak
2. How dangerous it can be to feel pressured to drop the price just because you're not great at dealing with silences.

Not sure if you can negotiate? Here's a little fun challenge for when you are shopping outside of work:

Step 1. In venues that are not fixed-price (i.e. don't choose a supermarket) challenge yourself to just ask if they are able to give you a discount. Do this on your next five purchases. No excuses, for each and every one of your next five purchases, ask if it is possible for them to give you a discount. If you do this with a friendly smile on your face, no one is going to bite your head off! This task is not about getting a discount, but about the confidence to ask for one!

Repeat step 1 for as long as it takes to get you feeling more confident with initiating a negotiation.

Step 2. For the next five purchases (again not in fixed-price venues) aim to get them to reduce their price. Count it as a win if you can get even just a penny off your purchase. If you want, make it fun and explain your request for a discount is because you are in a competition (as you are in a competition – a competition with the voice inside your head!).

Repeat step 2 for as long as it takes for you to find the right way to ask for a reduction and until such time as you are repeatedly getting the response from vendors that you are seeking.

Step 3. For the next five purchases (again, not in a fixed price venue), approach the task slightly differently. When you seek to make the purchase, you should already have in mind where else you might go to buy this item should you not be able to buy it here at the price you are seeking. Be prepared to walk away. Say that you are looking to buy xyz and are looking to find out where you can obtain the best price. Ask what the best price they can offer you is. Walk away if they do not offer you a discount.

low-hanging fruit

I'm sure you are all aware of the concept of low-hanging fruit. But it's easy to get caught up in our own ideas and crises that we forget about the low hanging fruit. For those of you who haven't come across this expression before, the low-hanging fruit refers to the sales that are easy to get, or the wins in business that are pretty much there for the taking.

Two scenarios ...

1. You have a day free. Do you go to a conference to widen your network or do you get on the phone to develop your relationships with those already in your network?
2. Sales are down. Do you come up with a plan to enter new markets, bring a new product or service to markets, think about diversifying or innovating? Or do you take out your existing customer list and identify where you might be missing opportunities for add on sales and referrals?

In business there are seldom any black and white answers but there are often easy ways and hard ways to achieve what we need to achieve. If only we were able to occasionally look up from what we are doing from time to time to see what the easier ways are.

The following two facts might help you decide where the 'low-hanging fruit' in the above scenarios probably is:

❖ Typically 80% of your sales will come from 20% of your customers.

❖ It often takes seven 'hits' of marketing for someone to first approach you with a view to buying.

It will therefore always be easier to seek to generate more revenue out of your existing customer base, than by seeking out potential new customers. That said, don't be so complacent that you don't have a strategy for attracting in new clients.

Here are some of the reasons why I think we don't 'look up' often enough in business to see if there is any low-hanging fruit:

- We've invested too much money pursuing one course of action so feel that looking up will distract us.
- We've invested too much emotionally in our current course of action to want to pursue other things before we have this one cracked.
- We are too busy fighting fires to remember to look up.
- We don't recognise the value of looking up/thinking time
- We lack people around us who feel able to challenge our current course of action.
- We are sticking our heads in the sand and don't want to know we are taking the wrong approach.

But if we do look up, here are a few ideas about what we can do to make sure we are in a position to grab all the low-hanging fruit available to us …

- Every time you or your team complete a sale, identify what if anything you could have done differently (offered more, identified add on sales, pricing, built the relationship more etc.).
- Remember that 80% of your business comes from just 20% of your clients, so work out who those great clients are and monitor what they are buying and when.
- Build in regular thinking time on business matters to provide an opportunity to review and amend what you do and what you sell.
- Review at least once each month where you are at, what is working, what you are missing.
- Brutally analyse each and every sale you lose.
- Be in contact on a very regular basis with your existing customers.
- Castigate yourself severely if ever it takes you more than 1 day to respond to a new client enquiry.
- Castigate yourself severely if anyone came into your shop but not once did you engage them in conversation to see what it was they were looking to buy.

- Educate your staff about add on sales, customer care, asking for the sale, asking for referrals etc and then aim to re-educate them at least once a month about some of these things.
- Know what your competitors don't deliver/offer and fill that gap.
- Ask for referrals continuously. But ask for them at the right time i.e. not when your customer is distracted with other stuff.

> Many retailers make huge amounts of money by selling us products we did not go into their stores to buy. From bottles of water and bars of chocolate at WH Smith who used to make their money from books, newspapers and stationery to insurance and phones from Tesco who used to sell us food. When I started my career it was reported that one electrical chain made more money in one year from selling extended warranties on its fridges, freezers and washing machines than it did on selling those white goods in the first place. These are easy sales. Your customers are already in the shop. They know the shop. Customers feel comfortable buying from them and then, at the final hurdle, customers are offered something that looks and feels like an easy extra purchase. What would it do to your business if you sold just one more thing to every customer that walked through your door ... the transformation to your turnover and profits can be dramatic.

sales mistakes

What are the common things so many of us do during the sales process that lose us sales and customers?

1. Lack of planning and research which can either make us look stupid in front of our potential new customer or can otherwise waste precious meeting time covering ground that really should have been covered before we arrived. Lack of planning just doesn't make us look professional or polished.

   For my part, I have noticed that sometimes I know more about the company than I actually let on as the prospect immediately begins to tell me about the organisation and I allow them to continue. The reason I do this is either because I want to hear it from the horse's mouth, or because I think it will sound rude to cut them off by saying I know it already. In hindsight, though, this may sometimes give the impression that I have not done my research.

2. Leaving voice mails asking the prospect to return our calls, sending emails asking the prospect to read and reply and allowing the client to lead the questioning. When we all have such busy days it is so easy to note that our to do list requires us to phone Miranda Mayhem to follow up a proposal. So we dial the number, get put through to voice mail then leave a message for Ms Mayhem to call us back. What on earth makes us think she will ever do that?

   So many of us need to learn that we have to stay in control of our client relationships which means that instead of asking Ms Mayhem to return our call, we leave a message saying when we will next call. In the same way, we can ask questions in our email, but we should end by saying how and when we will follow up with them.

   Its not good enough to tick the job off on our to do list and wait for the prospect to call or email us back.

a little story:

If you are feeling like there is an awful lot to do in setting up and running a business, do not despair. Consider yourself and your business a work in progress!

Earlier this year I wanted to buy a new car. I love my current car and in fact have purchased the same make and model twice already in the past ten years, but I wanted a new one. I arranged an appointment and on the due date went to the swish garage that sells this particular car and met with the sales manager, telling him exactly what I wanted. He said he would email me a quote. I waited exactly one week before first chasing. After chasing several times by phone a quote then came through by email from someone who presumably was an assistant to the sales manager I had met. Unfortunately, the information provided wasn't complete and not in line with what I had asked for, so I asked for further details. This is what then came through by email:

Hi Helen,

As agreed I have put together an example quote relating to the car I sent over to you the other day. The Price includes a discount approaching 6500 off the List price.

I realise this may not be what you want but it is a good starting point to spur you on to setting up a meeting with me to fine tune the details.

Please call me when you can to arrange an appointment.

Kind regards

Tom

So if an international giant such as this car company, with presumably extremely expensive sales training in place, has members of its sales teams sending out emails saying 'I realise this may not be what you want … please call me when you can to arrange an appointment' you might take some comfort in knowing that it is not just small businesses that make mistakes with sales.

Inevitably I did not call him to make an appointment, but what is unbelievable is that neither has he ever called me to follow up.

3. Organisation – another mistake is to be badly organised. Not to turn up on time, to get the day wrong, the venue wrong, forget the name of the person we are meeting with, not bring the right literature with us, fail to read the brief, fail to send a proposal to them within the timescale we promised to them, and failing to call them when we said we would call them.

   From a perception point of view, if we cannot organise ourselves at this stage of the sales process, how on earth will be sort ourselves out further down the line when they are waiting for us to deliver?

4. Being too busy selling ourselves to listen to what it is they want to buy from us. If we enter a meeting feeling that it will be a hard sell, it is probably going to impact on the way we approach the meeting. We will probably feel compelled to try to persuade them as to why they should buy from us, why our prices are competitive, why we do well in business, why others won't provide such a great product or service. But during all this time of selling ourselves, the reality is that we are not listening to what the clients wants from us. Many of us would do better to sell less and listen more. A quote I quite like is: 'We have two ears and one mouth and we should remember this when communicating, aiming to spend twice as much time listening as speaking.'

5. Not asking. It has been one of my many mistakes over the years not to ask for the business and not to ask for the referrals. I see others doing this too. We submit proposals or show prospects what we can do and we assume that they will understand that we are asking for the business. We also do a good job and assume that if they have a referral to pass our way, they will do just that because we have done a good job for them. This is not the case, though. Many of us could do better if we ask for the sale more often (or ask what it is we can do to get the sale) and if we ask for the referrals more often.

6. Putting sales activity off. I see this one so often. You get busy at work and you need to deliver to clients, so all of your time and energy goes into client delivery; but then, when the busy time is over, you look up and realise that your pipeline and your sales have dried up. You have to learn to be really disciplined and to make sure that even during busy times you still schedule in sales meetings and sales activities to keep that pipeline going.

Just to finish this section I thought I would share with you a great story I came across some years ago. I have no idea who first came up with it which is a shame as I can't credit them with it, but this is perhaps the ultimate 'sales mistake' – a lack of belief in your own gut instinct.

the hot dog story

A man lived by the side of the road and sold hot dogs.

He was hard of hearing so he had no radio.

He had trouble with his eyes so he read no newspapers.

But he sold good hot dogs.

He put up a sign on the highway telling how good they were.

He stood at the side of the road and cried, 'Buy a hot dog mister.'

And people bought.

He increased his meat and bun orders.

He bought a bigger stove to take care of his trade.

He got his son home from college to help him.

But then something happened ...

His son said: 'Father haven't you heard the news?

There's a big recession on.

The unemployment situation is terrible.

The energy situation is worse.'

Whereupon the father thought 'Well my son has been to college.

He reads the papers and listens to the radio, and he ought to know.'

So his father cut down on his meat and bun order.

Took down his advertising signs.

And no longer bothered to stand on the highway to sell hot dogs.

And his hot dog sales fell almost overnight.

'You're right son,' the father said to the boy.

'We are certainly in the middle of a great recession.'

You are always going to make some mistakes with sales, but if you want to minimise mistakes, write one thing here that you will focus on to keep you on track:

NOTES

CHAPTER NINE

finance

- 33% women would set up in business if they weren't so afraid of failure.
- Concern about debt is one of women's biggest fear factors.

I know, I know, this isn't the chapter you have been looking forward to, but tough! Finance can't be avoided so please don't skip this section, even if you are a seasoned financial professional. I promise I won't go into much detail at all but there are some things I want to flag up with you.

cash flow

Cash flow is king. It doesn't matter how much profit you make, if you run out of cash you are sunk.

There is a tendency for people setting up a small venture of their own to pretty much spend what they make, just putting a little to one side for the taxman! But this is a disaster waiting to happen or at the very least, will mean that you will never have the funds to invest in growth and without growth, most businesses wither and die.

No-one ever suggested saving money to me. If we ever had any excess we either reinvested it for growth or we used it to pay off the mortgage on our house or buy a new car. But not doing this nearly killed my business during the recession. If from day one you put a little of your monthly profit into a savings account you will accrue money for a rainy day ... or for the day your largest client fails to pay you, or when a client goes bust on you, or when a major corporate client suddenly informs you they will pay in 120 days rather than the thirty you agreed, or when the next recession hits.

Lack of money in the bank hit me hard during the last recession. Who could have predicted sales falling by 30% two years running? It was unprecedented. But it happened.

I have heard it recommended that you should aim to have savings in your business equivalent to around one year's turnover. That's huge for most start-ups, but it's important, so try to put money aside as soon as you begin to trade.

keeping good accounts

It might seem obvious to many of you, but regular accounting is also essential. At least once a month you need to know where you are with cash flow, sales, costs and of course profit (or loss).This means setting up the necessary spreadsheets using Excel or similar or otherwise investing in accounts software – and using it!

Many women admit to having low confidence with business finances. If you are one of them, you are not alone! I know women who would agree that poor financial knowledge has held back the growth of their business. If you are likely to be one of those who struggle with business finance, then I recommend you invest in a teach-yourself book, or attend a training course. Not being able to gasp your own essential finances is a non-starter if you want to own a business. The consequences of messing up are just too great.

You don't have to be a financial whizz, though! Interestingly I never made much more than 15% on a maths test until somehow I scraped through my basic maths exam at the age of sixteen. But when it comes to the maths in my own business, I've always been able to do that. When maths comes alive – when it's your own money – you might just find you weren't the high school maths dunce your teacher said you were! The key, though, is to learn how to set up and use a spreadsheet, so get yourself on a course. This is a must. Shall I repeat that? This is not an option! Go book yourself onto a one-day course right now!

In terms of outsourcing your finances to someone who knows what they are doing, well there are three types of person you might consider:

- a bookkeeper
- a finance director
- an accountant

Whilst I have always kept our actual invoicing and credit control (debt collection!) activities in-house, I have always had a bookkeeper. Someone who comes in every month to keep my books straight, produce my financial reports, do my staff payroll, tell me what I need to pay in tax and identify early on if there any discrepancies or errors on invoices. Essentially this person keeps me in order for just a few hundred pounds a month.

I have also always had an accountant, but tend to only see them for my formal end-of-year accounts, so they are usually a one-off annual cost. At the end of the year my bookkeeper liaises with the accountant and hey presto, all being well a month or so later my formal annual accounts are done. With no blood, sweat or tears on my part. Now that's what I call a good result!

From time to time I have also invested in a finance director. Not employed by me, but usually someone who has set up on their own and who now supports various companies. A finance director is the odd man out here as they are not just about compliance. Instead a good finance director will be commercially minded, they will be able to show you how to use your financial information to build your business.

Finance directors can help you put together information for budgeting, or a business sale, acquisition, or a cash flow forecast. More senior and experienced than a bookkeeper, the finance director can turn your financial information into something really useful and valuable to enable you to make good business decisions. Perhaps not required in the early years, this is someone worth investing in when you are ready to take your business out of start-up and into high growth mode. If that is what you want to do.

I have, though, come across numerous small businesses that have never needed to invest in a finance director. And even in high growth businesses it should be some years before you need to employ one directly.

cash and how it can impact on your accounting

Many businesses nowadays never see any cash. Particularly those that are B2B (business to business) rather than B2C (business to consumer). However, those that do can get into a pickle more quickly than those that get paid by cheque or direct into the bank.

Perhaps your business feels like a hobby, so what's the harm in spending some of your business cash in the supermarket rather than banking it? Or perhaps you are determined for your accounts to show the smallest possible profit in order to minimise any tax bill? Well, it's up to you of course – although in many countries you are effectively behaving illegally in not keeping full accounts and not declaring all your earnings for tax purposes.

There are two downsides though:

1. How can you sit back at the end of the year and tell yourself how well you have done if you don't really know what your turnover has been because money has been slipped out of the business left, right and centre?

2. And how can you grow the business and properly plan for that growth when you don't know what you actually turned over this past year?

I would also ask you how anyone will view you as running a serious business if you don't even do the most basic accounting. It smacks of you earning a little pin money and being a bit half-hearted about it all. Is that what you want?

I know someone who bakes cakes and sells them to shops, market stalls and online. The impression I get is that she is doing well and she now employs others on a part time basis to bake for her. Whenever I ask her though she is never really sure whether she is making any money, i.e. profit.

The reason for this is that when she shops for ingredients she often also buys things for her household. This results in her receipts being a mess. When she is paid in cash, some of it she banks and some if it she doesn't. When she works out her profit she never includes her own time, or if she does she includes time for baking but not for shopping. She also exchanges some services with friends – i.e. you do my website I'll bake you some cakes.

So at the end of the year no one can ever tell her if her business is loss-making or profit-making.

And I know hundreds of people like this who run hobby businesses or one-man bands but they are never able to congratulate themselves on what they have achieved as they are not really sure what they have achieved; they are not able to identify opportunities for efficiency or growth as they lack sensible financial information on what things are costing them and what their profit margins on their different products or services are. Furthermore, in the case of two of them they have not been able to convince their relatively unsupportive husbands that their business is valuable as it brings real (as opposed to pin) money into the household.

If you are setting up in business and intend to work from home, I recommend you think about how you will account for these business costs:

- your time (what is your hourly rate?)
- home equipment
- home energy and utilities (electricity, gas, water etc.)
- home storage space
- vehicle upkeep and mileage
- internet and telephone costs

It is so easy for accounts to get into a real pickle. You plan on doing them at the end of the month, but somehow something happens, and three months later you really can't remember what invoice was for what or what mileage you clocked up three months earlier. To avoid the stress of all of this, I recommend that what you do is be disciplined enough to log at the end of each day cash in, money paid directly into your bank account, money you have spent (keep invoices stored carefully in chronological order) and your time.

time is money

logging

Many who work from home, particularly those who do hours around family commitments, don't have the luxury of easy to log hours. You don't start at 8 am, have forty-five minutes for lunch and then finish at 5 pm each day. Usually, it's a lot more haphazard than that, so if you need or want to understand the value of the time you are putting into your own business, you need to log. This is a business you are running, not a stall at a local charity fair.

timesheets

Many in the service sector fill in daily timesheets. Often this is to be able to identify what to bill clients. However, it is a great discipline for someone just setting up in business.

Create a timesheet that enables you to log your time by units of fifteen minutes or half an hour. Have a code for time you bill directly to clients, time you spend on admin, time you spend on marketing and sales, time you spend manufacturing and for 'non time', i.e. all the time you spend messing about on the itty bits!

In the business I run we have always strived for around 65% productivity. That means that those in my business who are employed to deliver a front line service are expected to bill around 65% of their time (that leaves 35% of time for things such as emails, toilet breaks, admin, customer service, sales management, drinks, team meetings etc.). I have come across businesses, though, that expect staff to bill 90% or more of their contracted hours. This inevitably means that team meetings and toilet visits tend to be inappropriately logged to different client accounts.

It is, of course, up to you what percentage of time you expect your staff to be directly involved on client billing, or operating the production line in your factory, or serving customers in your shop. What is crucial is that you know what you expect and that your staff understand your expectations too.

And even for those of you who do not bill hours to the client, again you need to decide what level of productivity you are seeking. If you employ someone to bake cakes or man a production line, do you expect fifteen minutes chat at the start and end of each shift, plus three hours per month off the job training and three hours a month for meetings? Or do you say that chat is off limits and any lost time for meetings has to be made up at the end of the day? Different things for different business cultures, so there are no rights or wrongs, you just have to decide what is appropriate for the business you have set up – and then make sure that you staff understand your expectations!

fraud

It might seem odd in a book about setting up in business to talk about fraud, but I've included it here because it's important and too many of us learn how to protect our businesses after the damage has been done. You can, though, protect your business from the outset if you just recognise that fraud is a real problem in business.

I know stacks of people who have been affected by fraud. From fraud of just a few hundred euros to fraud running into the hundreds of thousands.

a few facts:

Employee-committed acts are the most common and most expensive type of fraud, accounting for more than half of all reported cases.

The Association of Certified Fraud Examiners: £300 billion per year in the UK is lost to internal fraud. Small businesses are most vulnerable, accounting for a whopping 80% of all internal fraud cases.

Many employers balk at the thought of spending £350 on a good quality pre-employment screening check to verify a candidate's CV, but compare this with the possible loss (average loss is 3% of turnover) and suddenly £350 looks good value.

Some of the major retailers report that loss of product to shoplifters is inconsequential compared to the loss to their own staff.

What is particularly horrifying is that many people do not think of stealing from a company as fraud. Also I have experience of the UK the police not being interested in supporting businesses by investigating fraud. A notable example of this was from a few years ago when a client of ours discovered around £150K had been stolen. However, despite the huge sum, on approaching the police they were stunned to be told, 'We don't do "fraud". Not enough resources for that.'

What has happened in society that theft from a company is virtually ignored whereas theft from a person is (hopefully) dealt with? But many companies are owned by one person. In fact in the UK I believe that 90% of SMEs (small and medium-sized enterprises) have fewer than ten staff, and I am sure many of these will be owned by one person. So it's not really theft from a company, but theft from a business owner – a person. However unfortunately that is not the approach that is taken by the law.

So when it comes to fraud, you, as the business owner, need to protect what is yours and safeguard against fraud.

The most common types of fraud I come across are:

From the little stuff ...

- Staff stealing your pens, staplers, ink cartridges, paper and stock.
- Staff taking a sickie and expecting you to pay a day's sick pay.
- Staff with access to petty cash or other cash siphoning a bit off.
- Staff fiddling their expenses.
- Staff who say they are working from home but who in fact are working for another employer or perhaps just taking an extra day's holiday.
- Staff spending their working hours on Facebook or Reddit.

To the big stuff ...

- Staff ordering stock through the company, but then selling it privately.
- Staff with access to your bank accounts stealing money from you.
- Staff selling your defunct stock on eBay.

- Senior staff systematically withdrawing funds from the business.
- Accounts or payroll staff either adding on fictitious people to the payroll or amending (upwards) their own salary details.

A starting point is being clear with staff about what you view as fraud. If you consider them taking a calculator home as theft, but they view that as just one of the perks of the job, then you need to set the standards with them. You should never assume they have the same views as you or even the same moral code as you, so setting standards is essential.

Have a clear policy on theft and fraud, set out clearly what you might consider to be theft or fraud, explain how you will deal with fraud.

Secondly, put in place independent audits. It is a mistake to ask your accounts manager to audit the work they themselves are doing. Trust is lovely, but it won't protect you from fraud. You should also be aware that the majority of fraud in businesses is perpetrated by those in senior positions, not by those in junior positions.

Management information is also essential. As a business owner you should cast your eye over figures and in time will know instantly if there are figures that look odd or that don't quite stack up. If something feels wrong, trust your instincts and be vigilant at all times.

So regular spot checks on staff absences, stock levels, expenses claims, invoices vs. monies paid out, bank balances, salaries, sales etc. In my business, it took me fifteen years to put it in place and it was really long overdue, but I now have a weekly report of monies in the bank account, monies due in, sales billed, invoices outstanding. One business owner I know gets this information on a daily basis to ensure she gets sight of any potential problems at the earliest possible moment.

setting up on a shoestring

I saw some research that suggested typical start-up costs for a new enterprise in the UK are around £20,000. However, many will be set up with far less given that 75% of businesses (2011 UK report by BIS) are run by sole traders (i.e. no staff and probably working from home).

I have also seen research which suggests that women tend to find their start-up capital either from their own savings or from close friends and family. It is well documented that women tend not to seek external financing either during the set up phase or whilst building the business up. This is in contrast to men, who often seem far more comfortable with the prospect of accessing external funding.

What is also clear from research is that many women initially set up in order to be able to work part time from home. Figures suggest that 35% of female enterprises are set up specifically to work around family commitments. I wouldn't therefore be surprised to find that if you really had to, you could set up with just a £1000 in today's environment if you are going to work from home with no staff – a computer, broadband connection and mobile phone are the essentials.

When I first set up I bought a computer, a printer, some paper and other office essentials. I paid £400 to the local Chamber of Commerce for a small database of their members for my first marketing mail shot and that was about it.

As with many women, though, I didn't exactly plan well as I had no business plan, no budget, no sales targets and I didn't record all my business expenses until the business got established. Crazy really as there is no point in spending money out of your purse but through lack of record-keeping and organisation, have no means of offsetting that against your turnover when you start to sell. That's just chucking money down the pan, but lots of us are far too informal and haphazard with our finances and record keeping when we first set up.

So if you are still in the planning stage of launching a business, how about you list here what you physically need to set up with on day one and also what you think you will spend in addition to this over the first six months. Treat this as a holiday packing list – i.e. put all your thoughts down now and then keep adding to it as more things occur to you.

NOTES

what i need for my fab new business:

1

2

3

4

5

6

7

8

9

10

Next to each item indicate whether it is essential or just nice to have.

If you choose to sort your items into the following sections, this list can then begin to form part of your business plan.

- ❖ premises (rent, rates, utilities, furniture etc.)
- ❖ office consumables (ink cartridges, paper etc.)
- ❖ technology (hardware, software and support)
- ❖ staff (salaries, associates, expenses, recruitment fees, recruitment advertising, training, plus employers NI ... (a UK tax on employers)
- ❖ compliance (insurances, bookkeeping, accountancy, legal fees, business registration, professional subscriptions, accreditations or certifications etc.)
- ❖ marketing and sales (design and printing of literature, website development and maintenance, purchase of mailing lists, attendance at networking, exhibiting at conferences, PR agency, advertising, photos, etc.)
- ❖ purchase of materials or goods to fulfil sales

Next to each item indicate if it is a one-off cost or a recurring cost. Indicate, if possible, which months you will need to pay for it.

Now be ruthless. This chapter is, after all, about setting up on a shoestring. What can your business really survive with in the first few months? Be really harsh with those items that are nice to have, but not need-to-have. By all means buy them, but every month you can delay buying them will help your cash flow in those first few months.

Now go through your nice-to-have items. Prioritise them so you know what you will buy first once you start to sell. I don't want you going mad and buying them all on the day you make your first sale! It is about being really strict with yourself until you have enough money coming in.

But perhaps I should own up here. I don't really want you to set your business up on a shoestring unless you really have to do that. I want you to set it up in such a way that it has the potential to be really successful and to grow. You don't have to go mad on spending, but equally you don't have to keep costs so low that your business ends up costing less than a manicure!

I have come to dislike the shoestring approach to setting up, as over the years these are the problems I have seen female entrepreneurs encounter further down the line:

websites. Using a 'wannabe' website designer who offers to do your website at such low cost you really can't refuse, but months after you needed it up and running it is still being developed, your 'wannabe' designer has failed to set it up as you need it to be set up, and you feel you lost control somewhere along the line on the design. So now you have lost the opportunity to market yourself over several months, you might have lost some sales, you are dissatisfied with what you have ended up with and you feel this is not portraying the image or information your fledgling business needs.

book keeping and accountancy. As a result of trying to do it yourself you end up in a financial pickle with perhaps even the taxman landing you with a bill you never expected and certainly can't pay. You might incur additional end-of-year accountancy fees to cover the time it takes to unravel your mess, and worse still you might not know where you are making money and where you are losing it, so effectively you have no real means of running your business properly. And the worst case scenario is that if you mess up with cash flow, you might even go bust before you have even really begun.

the legal stuff. I have seen people drafting their own legal documents (employment contracts, terms of business, e-commerce agreements etc.) and getting into an enormous pickle with some of these. Perhaps you find out that the employment contract you downloaded as a freebie is missing essential information such as a Business Protection Clause, meaning your staff can leave you and take your clients with them, or perhaps the terms of business you drew up failed to state the means by which any trade disputes would be resolved.

The problem with legal documents is that you usually only get to find out what you have missed out or what clauses you have messed up when you encounter your first problem. But at that point it could cost you thousands (or tens of thousands) to resolve satisfactorily. It might even mean you have to write off certain debts or pay out compensation.

The Internet is full of free documents to download, but if you do download them, please, please remember that often the people drawing them up in the first place will never have had their own money and effort invested in their own business. What I am saying, therefore, is that for you the stakes are so much higher. You have no employer to bail you out of a hole and you can't just resign and move onto another job if things get sticky. So by all means take risks with legal documents, but don't take crazy risks that will cost you a whole pile of money to sort out when things go wrong.

staff. I can't speak here for all countries of the world, but in Europe and many other countries, small employers have no exemption from the prevailing employment law. As a new business, you therefore have to toe the line just as any other employer must do and no-one will go easy on you just because you are setting up and haven't yet put all the formalities in place you really should have done. Also pleading ignorance of the law is not acceptable and will not go in your favour.

This is where you need to invest in a bit of learning for yourself. You don't need to know everything about employing people, but you do need to know the basics both for compliance reasons and also because that is just good management.

recruitment. Start-ups often recruit from their existing base of associates and friends rather than from an agency. This can result in you getting some good staff. Its always good to work with people you already know, but occasionally this practice means that you are not recruiting the best available person for the job.

an informal relationship. If you choose to be really informal with your first employee then bear in mind that they might be informal with you and one consequence of that might be they leave you at a moment's notice rather than give you any warning. If you don't pay them holidays or permit holidays then (if you are based in Europe and subject to EU law) that could, in due course, cost you dear.

employment status. If you choose to 'employ' your worker(s) on a self-employed basis (e.g. associate or contractor) be aware that whilst this is good for your cash flow and might save on taxes and employee benefits, it might also expose your business as they may be less loyal, less inclined to protect your company secrets and information, less aware of who all your clients are and how they like to be treated and less inclined to do you favours (such as work longer hours) when you next have a crisis.

sales, marketing, PR and SEO (search engine optimisation). Stinting on the marketing and advertising of your business might seem like good cost control but it is widely accepted that spending on these areas can support faster business growth. The question is whether you are happy to just rely on word of mouth, a bit of internet exposure and some passing trade or would you like to hit the world with a bang? If you want significant business growth then you need to budget for marketing and advertising. You need to get your business name and products out there and widely known and stinting now, could hamper your future growth prospects.

friends and family. Many draw on the financial resources of their family and friends when setting up, and we turn to them too when seeking to save costs. It is not unusual to find family members doing admin, bookkeeping, website design, sales calls, marketing design, business plan development etc. Be careful, though, not to use people who have no clue what you trying to achieve, why you are trying to achieve it, what your business values are, what your vision is, what your tastes/style are etc., because they will end up doing only half a job for you and ultimately that just wastes time.

So use family and friends when you have checked that they can really deliver what you need. You might even need to learn to say 'no' to those who are really well intentioned and think they can help, but in fact they can't really deliver what you need it in the way you need it. Be grateful for their support, but learn to say no!

you. I have talked elsewhere in this book of the need to value your own time. By this I mean 1) place a monetary value on each hour of your time and 2) value your time generally as you do not have an infinite number of hours in each day – much as you would like to. Not valuing my time has been one of my big mistakes over the years.

From a monetary point of view, when someone says to you 'How much do you pay yourself?' don't just say 'Nothing really, but I'll be rich one day' or 'Not much now, but I will one day soon'. I know so many women who do that.

Equally, in respect of valuing your time generally, don't convince yourself that it saves money if you do a job yourself rather than outsource it. What you need to do is set yourself an hourly rate. Do this by working out what it would cost a large firm to employ you to do what you do. And no! Don't go undervaluing yourself or getting all bashful, as women so often do that.

If you decide that the market rate for your time is £60 per hour (this might not be the same as the rate at which you bill your clients if that is what you do), you now have a starting point for assessing whether it is sensible to do a job yourself or outsource it to a professional. Consider the real cost if you spend ten hours with your wannabe website developer explaining for the millionth time what it is you want them to do for you. If you were to pay an additional £1000 to an experienced web developer, but save yourself thirty hours, is that a good investment? So don't underestimate the cost of your time when seeking to cut costs elsewhere. It is all a balancing act – particularly in those early days when you have no money coming in. Just remember that it is nonsensical to cut costs in one place only to have to spend more elsewhere.

'shoestring' attitudes that inhibit business growth

not attracting new clients in

- ❖ Lack of a good website means that some might pass you by as you are not visible enough. Alternatively, perhaps your website makes you look like too much like a one person outfit (or business start-up) which can make buyers worried about whether you will be around next week.

- ❖ Poor photos on your website or poor quality images in your marketing material smack of a business that is not a quality business. Even if quality is not essential, if you are selling products online and your buyers can't see good pictures, they will probably move onto the next website where they can see what they are buying.

- ❖ Looking like you are a start-up (the way you talk, market yourself, what you drive, a half-hearted website, no business polish, no branding, no client list) will mean that your clients expect 'start-up' bargain rates which could have a disastrous affect on your profit margins.

- ❖ Printing your own marketing literature rather than getting it properly printed will always result in you looking 'homemade' and could mean you lose some potentially good business.

not keeping on board your existing clients

- ❖ Lack of management information means you don't know who your best clients are and what they are buying so how do you know what to promote and who to promote it to.

- ❖ If you are already very busy but choose to delay recruiting staff to service your customers, this could result in you letting down and losing the customers you have.

- ❖ Not paying for a telephone answering service could result in your clients and suppliers feeling that they are forever leaving messages and never have any idea how quickly you will be able to return their call. Will they lose confidence?

There is no one rule that fits every situation, though. You will be the best person to know what you could lose out on if you cut just one too many corners in seeking to keep costs down.

advice on working with financial investors

Just as a final section on Finance, I asked a friend of mine, Scott Dougan, who runs investment business Mense Investments what advice he would give to anyone thinking about seeking financial investment. Here is Scott's advice:

working with investors

At some point in almost every business there comes a moment when there is a need for an injection of cash. There are of course commercial sources of short-term funds but for long-term growth its best to have long-term funding and that usually means an investor. Before you even think about how much you need and how much the business is worth, give these matters some serious consideration:

1. stick with the business plan

Your business plan is what sets out your strategy for success. It will show not only what you will achieve, but more importantly how you will achieve it, with the resources, both financial and human, that you will need to do it. This plan is what will attract your potential investor so it's important to prepare it well and stick with it. Most businesses fail when they don't stick with the plan or forget to revisit it when circumstances change. That is because they don't re-plan their resources when changes take place and so become either over- or under-resourced, and therefore unable to deliver their plan.

2. pick the right partner

Each investor will have their own appetite for risk and reward, and you need to ensure that your goals match. Some partners are in it for the long term and some less so. Plus, consider what they would want out of the business if, say, you had to try raise further capital?

Would they be happy with another partner or a diluted stake in the business? Remember you have to work closely with your partner for a long period of time, so be sure you feel you can work with them. Even long-term relationships can falter and even cause total failure of the business. The self-tan brand favoured by celebrities, Fake Bake, went into administration recently because the key partners couldn't agree a way forward.

3. know how much control you wish to give up

Most of the time when you are looking for investment you are 'selling' a share of your business. You need to be comfortable with knowing how much of your 'control' you are selling, as an investor will want a say in how their money is being spent! Perhaps the investor brings a certain expertise that you don't have, in which case selling more of the business could entice him/her and also give you a greater opportunity for success. No matter what you intend to sell, and whether you remain a controlling interest or not, any relationship with an investor is a partnership and you need to feel you can work with this person. You need to also keep in mind that certain decisions (generally on matters set out by company law) can be blocked by the investor even if s/he has only 25% of the business.

4. agree an exit strategy

Critical when considering an investor is knowing when they are likely to want a return on their investment and want to sell out. It is vital that it matches your own timetable and also who you are likely to sell to. Unless you do agree this up front the running of the business can be affected dramatically as you look to disentangle yourself from the business relationship with your investor. Even 'family investors' can't be guaranteed to want the same as you. Ultimo lingerie supremo Michele Mone discovered that not only did her newly separated husband want bought out before the business was due to be sold but also that he had one extra share than her which meant she wasn't in full control of the business. Fortunately for her she found an investor to resolve her issue.

5. keep it formal

No matter how friendly you wish your business style to be or how much you feel you can trust your potential partner you can be sure that something will come along that will challenge the relationship, be it exit strategy, business strategy or, as it usually is, distribution of money. With that in mind it is always recommended that you take formal advice and have any investment, shares, roles and responsibilities made clear to both parties either by way of an investment agreement or shareholders' agreement. It may seem odd to debate how things may go in case of a failure, before you've started the relationship, but its best to do it for the protection of both parties.

CHAPTER TEN

focus on you!

Moving away from finance you may be relieved to see we now turn our attention to You. You are the centrepiece of your business. Your business would not exist without you. So this chapter is all about you!

I have probably never met you, but in the following sections I set out a few of my thoughts based on the entrepreneurs I have met. I suggest you read those sections that you find of most interest.

your supporters – how supportive are they really?

In Chapter One we looked at ambition and talked a little about who can support you in business. Perhaps now you have done some more thinking about the challenges in business, you should revisit those pages to see if any of your views have changed.

I won't duplicate any of that section here, but there are two points I want to raise:

1. Your supporters will change over time – at different stages of your business venture you will need different kinds of support. So accept right from the outset that your closest supporters will need to change as you and your business grow. It may be worth your while to keep an eye out while you are networking for people who might be good supporters as your business grows..

    Stage one supporters: You might be looking for those who will encourage you, boost your self esteem, say how proud they are of you, offer ideas and be a sounding board.

    Stage two supporters: You might need supporters who can give you constructive feedback, help out with the practical stuff such as child care, listen when you want to talk after a tough day, lend you some money, talk through your ideas.

    Stage three supporters: As the business is set up and moving forward, you might need supporters who have experienced some of the challenges you are now facing, such as creating websites, dealing with accountants, procurement, designing marketing literature, developing distribution channels etc.

    Stage four supporters: Again, if at some point you decide to move your business up a gear and aim for high growth, your supporters may need to change. At this point for me I joined a number of groups designed to specifically support women seeking high growth, namely WE Connect, Women Presidents' Organisation and United Succes. It was at this stage that it really came home to me that within my existing network there were very few who had any understanding of the issues I was facing or that were in a position to support me.

2. Recognising when people who say they are supportive are not really supportive at all. Do any of your supporters ever use phrases like these:

- I so admire what you are doing, but you are up against such competition.
- You are a great example to us all, but are your children okay with it?
- I knew your were ambitious, but I hardly see you any more.
- Wow, you are achieving so much, next you'll be wanting to travel the world.

❖ You are great at what you do, but don't neglect us, will you?

Sometimes it's not that they are intentionally not supportive, but the build-up of comments that suggest you are too ambitious, forgetting your friends, neglecting your kids, competing with the 'big boys' can all really undermine self-confidence. And whatever you do, when venturing into new territories, you cannot afford to be around people who, for whatever reason, undermine your self-confidence.

Other kinds of non supportive support (!) include saying they are supportive but:

❖ never helping out with childcare (and making you feel bad for asking!);
❖ beginning to exclude you from social events and friendship groups;
❖ making snide comments when you are late for an event or the school pick up;
❖ expecting you to do a full day of housework and childcare as well as running your business;
❖ huffing and puffing about why the dinner isn't on the table when your other half walks in;
❖ continually being on your case about what you haven't done;
❖ continually commenting about what you are not so great at rather than what you are good at;
❖ asking you if at any point you are going to give it all up; and
❖ logging how many nights you have been away from home or how many business trips you have been on.

The list could be endless, but as both men and women with a few years on the clock all know, our confidence can be massively undermined if there are people near us who continually 'pick' at us, perhaps even whilst telling us that they love us and support us.

It's a shocking thing to do, but perhaps an important thing to do, so look around you and ask yourself which of your supporters has every faith in you and your ability to run this business and succeed in your ambitions, versus who is really just waiting for you to say you can't do it or admit it is too much. Sometimes it's because they love you and they don't want to see you hurt or overworked. At other times, though, it might occur because if you succeed, what will that say about them? But that's okay, you just need to know that's the way it is and make sure you surround yourself with supporters who are 100% behind you, then pull out all the stops to achieve your goals!

growing your business and growing your skills

> I like this quote although I confess to not knowing where it came from originally:
>
> 'If you always do what you've always done,
> you'll always get what you've always got.'
>
> Is it time for you to learn new skills?

As our businesses grow and develop we need to develop our skills and knowledge too. I sometimes feel that despite seventeen years of learning I still don't know anywhere near enough to be able to set up or run a business! Perhaps in the early years ignorance was bliss and I didn't worry about what I didn't know I should be worrying about!

One of the greatest challenges for many of us is developing good skills to manage and lead people. In my seventeen or more years of running an HR consultancy I can count on one hand the number of natural born leaders I have come across. In my experience, most good leaders have had to learn how to successfully manage and lead their staff and as their teams get larger they sometimes have to run to keep up with the different demands! But it doesn't matter if you are still developing your skills, just as long as you keep learning and trying.

I know a business owner who has been running a business for many years. I got to know him really well at one point as the business was struggling during a period of significant change; staff were leaving and a succession of employee grievances had been raised. His staff said he listened but never heard, that he dumped rather than delegated, that he told but never asked, and that he communicated, but usually too little and too late.

He asked me for some coaching. However, in our sessions he listened but did not hear, he said that he delegated rather than dumped, but his staff needed to organise themselves better to do the work; he told me the problem was not him but caused by others not doing what they should or not being up to the task, and he repeatedly told me that he was a brilliant communicator. Needless to say the coaching didn't get far and personally I feel that if he is not prepared to listen, learn and develop himself then perhaps he is at the limits of his potential as a business leader.

If anyone ever tells you that running a business is easy, then my first piece of advice to you is 'don't listen to them'. In fact there is nothing harder than running your own business. The demands on you and the pressure on you to develop so many skills is enormous. That doesn't mean you shouldn't give it a go, though; just don't be complacent about the need to develop yourself and your skills – continually.

But returning to my impatient, frustrated but ego-driven business owner, if your staff perceive you as not listening to them, dumping work on them, telling them rather than asking and keeping them in the dark on important matters, it doesn't matter whether you think they are wrong because what you have to deal with are their perceptions of you and what you are doing.

You can't say to someone that their perception of you is wrong. Their perception is their perception and that is what you have to deal with if you are the business leader and you wish to move things forward.
As the leader you can't deny, blame or negate. In other words you can't blame others for what goes wrong; you can't deny other people's perceptions that things are going wrong and you can't negate other people's feelings by telling them they should not feel that way.

But whether you are setting up as a sole trader or with a view to employing others, what is crucial is that from day one you put time and effort into developing your skills. And developing your skills needs to be a lifelong endeavour, not just something you do once and then sit back waiting for your business to become successful.

developing your own skill set and knowledge

When I speak to girls and women's business groups about female entrepreneurship, these are the eight key skills and traits I suggest we all need to succeed in our ventures:

- You need to be a self-starter.
- You have to be able to be an independent thinker.
- Being financially responsible is crucial.
- Knowing how to innovate in business is essential
- You have to feel comfortable with risk.
- It is important that you enjoy hard work.
- You need to be determined.
- Resilience (being able to pick yourself up after it has gone wrong) is key.

I will look briefly at all these skills and traits below.

a self-starter

You cannot hang around waiting for someone else to show you how to do something, nag you to get out of bed in the morning, or hand you the keys to your first office. You have to initiate these things yourself.

If you are not a natural self-starter, then the only thing I can suggest is to find something that motivates you so strongly that you will become a self-starter. You are going to have to be really, really hungry to achieve though.

In my experience people who have spent a lifetime working for a large company can find it really hard to become a self-starter. They have learnt to wait for someone else to write the business strategy, for someone else to make the sales, someone else to think of where to take the business next. Many roles in large companies are so reactive that the incumbents have forgotten (or never learnt) how to self-start. This doesn't mean they can never become a self-starter, just that it might be something they have to work harder at before it becomes second nature.

an independent thinker

If you wait for others to come up with ideas, if you prefer to follow the pack rather than lead it, if you feel uncomfortable operating differently to others, or if you find it hard to question or examine what you are told, you may struggle to run your own enterprise. You need to have your own opinions, know your own mind and be your own person.

If you are not currently much of an independent thinker, then I see no reason why you cannot train yourself to question more, to come up with more of your own ideas etc. This might be a matter of self-discipline in continually reminding yourself that developing independent thinking skills is critical if you are to achieve your goals.

I know a wonderful woman who set up in business. In her first two years she effectively copied what someone else was doing. She did it very successfully and was helped by the fact that she used to be a client of the other business so knew how they worked, what they sold and at what price. But a few years down the line she started to struggle. Her business model was stagnant and she didn't seem to have the skills to rethink what she was doing and work out how to change it to move with the market. After four years she gave up her business and moved back into a corporate role. The lesson for me was that anyone can copy a successful company, but to grow and develop your own successful company at some point, you have got to start having ideas of your own.

financially responsible

In the initial stages you will have suppliers to pay and if you fail to pay them, that in turn could affect their ability to pay *their* suppliers. Business in this world has got to be sustainable, and that means that you need to be aware of what the impact might be on others if you are not financially responsible.

I do know some people who take the view that if you let down one supplier, there will always be another to take their place and in some markets this might be the case. For the most part though, taking a short-term view in business and treating others badly, will eventually come back to bite you in the bottom.

In my current business we have one client who once wrote to us to say that his business has gone into liquidation and therefore he wouldn't be able to pay our bill – ever. By chance we found out a few months later that the business had not gone into liquidation at all. So we pursued our bill by going to his premises and demanding a cheque. We never expected to deal with him again but about twelve months later he approached us and said that he needed more HR support. We said that we would only provide it if he paid in advance – for ever. So now we get our money in advance and he loses out because our advice to him is delayed because we always insist his money clears our bank first. He also is our only client to pay in advance. Overall, his behaviour breached the trust that needs to exist and that always has consequences.

innovative and creative

Lots of people ask me about this one. It is my belief that the business world is perhaps changing faster than we have ever experienced before. It might be a time will come when the pace of change slows down, but I doubt it. Technology, of course, is driving much of this change. However, there are numerous other factors at play. I gave you some quotes earlier on in this book about innovation and change; you might want to go back and take another look at those to provide you with an opportunity to think about the need to be open minded, and open to possibilities.

But quotes aside, if your business is to keep up with changing times, then you need to be innovating and creating within your own business to drive change internally. Stop changing and you stop growing. Stop growing and you wither and die.

If you are interested in innovation around the world, I have included at the back of this book a snippet from the 2013 GII (Global Innovation Index). Switzerland comes top yet again and I am very proud that of the 142 countries surveyed, the UK comes in at number 3.

But returning to innovation for your businesses, one thing that I have felt sorry about over the years is the state of some of the family-owned shops on the high street. I wonder if some family-owned businesses don't seek external support and external ideas often enough. Relying on family is great, but not if it means you miss out on bringing in fresh ideas or seeing how the world is changing around you.

With some of these shops, you walk past them year after year and you might even go in and buy something occasionally. But then one day you stop to look in the window and you see that they have no customers and that the reason they have no customers is that they look jaded and old fashioned. It could be a jewellery shop, a shoe shop or it could be a hardware store but if they, or any of us, stop changing, stop bringing in new products or services, or never take time out to rethink how we sell and market ourselves, then in time others will look in our 'shop window' and decide not to enter. It doesn't matter how great you used to be, you have to continually move forward in business.

But for those of you who feel this is not one of your strengths, then have no fear! You can learn to be innovative and you can learn how to draw out your inner creativity. I run workshops on this and I am sure others do too, so if this one is difficult for you, then I suggest you find someone who can help.

not risk averse

I talk elsewhere in this book about risk. It's a big issue for women. It's a big issue for many men too, but my observation over the years would be that it's a bigger issue for women.

I read a report a few years ago that suggested that a third of women would set up in business if they weren't so afraid of financial debt. Others, of course, fear failure and others yet fear venturing into the unknown without corporate safety nets in place.

But whilst it is sensible to have some fear – as this will ensure you are not reckless – some people are just not cut out for risks such as you face in business. You launch a new product and there are no guarantees it won't sink without trace. You set up a new business and there is no guarantee of success. You take on a member of staff and there are no guarantees they will not defraud you. You borrow £100K and there is no certainty you will ever be able to pay it back. The list of risk factors goes on and on. And risk aversion can cause serious stress which in turn badly damages health and wellbeing. I don't therefore think this is a skill or trait to be developed. Either you are comfortable with risk or you are not.

Serious risk aversion also can kill a business. I have encountered many women paralysed with fear of what might go wrong. Sometimes women want to set up in business, but three years after we first spoke they are still paralysed by fear. I have seen others who are already in business but who take so long to make a decision, just in case it is the wrong decision, that the market has moved on and they have lost their opportunity.

hard-working

If I am really truthful, I do know a couple of business owners who aren't hard-working. They had a great idea for a niche product and are milking it for all its worth and much of the day to day work is offloaded onto somebody else. They have no business once this niche product opportunity is exhausted though.

I also know a few who spend three months or more each year sailing around the Caribbean, but the reality is that all of these worked their socks off in the early years of their business and are now enjoying the return.

The reality, of course, is that most business owners work really hard. And when they are not working in the business they are thinking about the business or otherwise networking hard at some trade show or on linked in. I spend hours in the swimming pool and length after length I plan my day, I write chapters in my head for this book, I work out what I need to say in our next team meeting, I plan my next public speech. I might be swimming, but it's constant thinking that keeps me moving forward. I suspect most other business owners are the same. Brains constantly whirring!

If you are averse to hard work, self-employment is probably not for you. I would recommend you try to sell this book to someone else to at least recoup your outlay!

determined

Very little that is good in life comes easily. For most things that we want we have to work really hard to attain them. Being successful in business is no different. Sometimes I find that women (and that includes me) lack the incredible single-minded focus that men can have in their careers. Our brains far too often are busy thinking about dinner, shopping, children, childcare, organising family events, organising our social lives, caring for elderly relatives, managing the household etc.

But whilst we are often not so single-minded and focused in business, women in business often make up for this with our determination. We dig our heels in and keep going, through thick and thin. And when its not working, we work out how to make it work, for no one else is going to sort it for us.

If you have this determination, then you will be great in business. If you don't have it, then you can choose to change, for I believe that determination is about mindset. It's not really a skill to develop, more a change that is required in your attitude, and we can, every one of us, always choose to change our attitude. Critically, though, you need to have a clear vision of what you are trying to achieve and why you are trying to achieve it in order to be determined enough to battle through. If you lack vision, you may well lack the drive required to demonstrate your determination.

As I am sure you already know, the attrition rate of new businesses is very high. I suspect this is the same all over the world. I expect some of the business failures occur as a result of the business owner not setting out with a clear vision and a clear plan so they then spend a year of so thrashing around like a dying fish desperately hoping that success will come all on its own. If you are determined to succeed in this business venture you are considering or have just set up, then as a starting point, take the time now to set out your vision and plan.

resilient

Eleanor Roosevelt once said that a woman is like a teabag – you never know how strong she is until you put her into hot water.

I have always loved that quote. It makes me very proud to be a woman that so many of us can be so strong for ourselves, our families and our businesses when life gets tough. But returning to resilience as a skill for entrepreneurs …

I have always thought of running a business as a bit like riding a roller coaster. There are immense highs and there are immense lows. Huge twists, stomach-churning drops and quite often you are carried along completely upside down. You might even be one of the unlucky few whose carriage comes off the track and you have to hope you come out of the wreck alive.

In business you have to know it is not always going to be an easy ride. It will be tough and at times it will feel unbelievably hard but the rewards, the highs, when you get it right are simply the best feeling in the world. No other job could compare. So if you want to take the roller-coaster ride, then know that you will need to be resilient. You can't get off when the going gets tough, you can't lose control when you are careering out of control upside down in your roller-coaster cart and you can't step out when the ride slows down. Either you join the ride and stay on it, or you don't get on at all.

But it's little by little, for when you set up and it's just you in one office with one desk and one phone, you only need a little resilience. Then slowly over the years as the customer base builds, the office gets bigger, you take on staff, your turnover grows, your resilience needs to grow with it. Stick with it and I bet that one day you will turn around and see that of all your family and friends you are one of them most resilient people you know!

a short story ...

Running your own business is tiring. Running a house and working with two young children is tiring. Being pregnant and having your third baby not long after setting up in business is a potential disaster! When this happened to me, I recruited someone to work alongside me while I was pregnant with my third child. I already had two children aged three and four and the plan was to get her in place so that I could take some maternity leave and re-energise but would still have a business to return to.

That first employee taught me much about business ... and how supportive women can be. She dumped me shortly before my baby was born, saying she wanted to spend more time with her teenage children before they grew up and left home. Time and money training her down the pan. My confidence dented. But you get these knocks in business and if you are to be a business woman you just have to learn to pick yourself up.

So I did. And on Thursday 1st July 1999 I went to the maternity unit at 8 am. Delivered my third baby by lunchtime, was home by tea time and back at my desk by Friday morning, baby in my arms.

And working from home has so many advantages. You can be pregnant and clients don't really know. You can be breastfeeding whilst on the telephone advising about a dismissal, you can deliver a seminar and then race home to feed your baby and change its nappy before responding to the morning's messages and you can catch forty winks in between jobs without anyone being any the wiser!

Perhaps a time will come, though, when you find the challenges too great and it would just be easier to give in and give up. If this is the case with you, here are some of my ideas to help you get back on track:

- Never give up; you are doing this for you and perhaps also your family, so giving up is not an option.

- By all means cry from time to time, but don't even think of apologising for that or apologising for the fact that women can get emotional at times. We should never have to pretend we don't get emotional and never apologise for when we do. If that makes someone feel uncomfortable … tough!

- Remember you are part of a movement. Fifty years ago few women around the world worked outside of the home or the domestic environment so this movement to create opportunities for female entrepreneurship is new and, as with all new movements, the ride will never be totally smooth, so expect a few rocks and crevices along the way.

- Have in mind that whatever you experience, some woman somewhere will have experienced worse.

- If men put you down and suggest you don't have what it takes to make it, ignore them; that is just their fear or ignorance talking.

- If women put you down, ignore them, it has traditionally been women's place in society to maintain the status quo and you are challenging that, so it is inevitable that they fear you, or fear your influence, so ignore them and carry on regardless.

- If you ever wonder whether you have what it takes, take heart as virtually all company owners, male and female, have these thoughts. You are entirely normal!

- ❖ If you have had a knock and don't know whether you can carry on, always allow yourself time to be emotional, but then your first action should be to return to your business plan. Rethink it, rewrite it or just remind yourself of it.

- ❖ And once you have a plan in mind, you can now carry on. Spend, spend, spend is not an option. You will be far more resilient as a person and as a business if you save a little of everything you earn so that you have reserves for tough times. So do this from day one.

- ❖ Never be embarrassed by failure. If your business venture fails then that is fine as long as you have learnt from what you did wrong. Then pick yourself up and set up your second business. If you look at many very successful business people, you will find that many of these have failed business ventures behind them. Failure is just indicative of the fact that you tried to do something that many others would not even have tried. So be courageous and try again.

leadership and humility

Beyond the skills and traits we have looked at so far, what other skills might you need to develop when your business is established and growing? Leadership is clearly one, but there are many others such as:

- developing your self-esteem and self-confidence
- financial understanding/confidence
- sales techniques
- marketing knowledge
- effective use of technology
- confident communication skills
- networking skills
- delegation skills
- staff management skills
- coaching skills
- motivating staff
- self-presentation skills
- formal presentation skills
- health and safety knowledge
- corporate governance knowledge

Would you prioritise any of these for needing your urgent attention? Please can I ask you to take the time now to put a tick against those you need to develop.

A tip: if you have felt tempted to tick more than five of these (and please don't tell me you have ticked all of them – that would be such a female thing to do!) then you need to be strict with yourself.

Be focused and aim to work on just one or two things at a time. So go back and choose no more than two!

Did you know that in business men tell their superior that they are ready for a promotion when they are around 80% competent in their current role? Women wait until they are 100% competent in their current role and have been for some time, before then asking their superior what else they might do to prepare themselves for a promotion.

Similarly, at interview, men will talk confidently about the 80% of the job spec that they can do and ignore the fact that they have no skills for the remaining 20% of the job spec. Women however, will spend most of the interview talking about the 20% of the role they cannot do.

Not surprisingly, women do exactly the same in business, which is why I know that about 50% of you reading this book will have ticked almost every single one of those skills I set out above. You will also be thinking about all the reasons why you don't have the skills for this business venture instead of thinking that you already have great skills and you will learn the rest as you go!

So let me say this really clearly, my lovely female readers, you do not need all of these skills to set up in business. What you need to do, though, is know what skills you need to develop if you are to run a growing business and then create a plan for yourself to ensure you develop them over the coming five to ten years.

But because it is such an essential skill and one that will be continuously developed across your career, let's take a brief look at leadership.

leadership –
how are you going to become a great leader?

In business there will be many occasions when others either criticise or praise your leadership skills. In running your own business, whether you like it or not and whether you have staff or not, others will see you as a leader. Typically they will have opinions on you based on:

- how you lead your staff;
- what impact your business has on the local (or wider) community; and
- how innovative or adventurous your friends, family and acquaintances view your enterprise.

If you are just starting out on your entrepreneurial journey it may be that you have not yet thought about what sort of leader you would like to be. If this is the case, then here are a few quotes to get you thinking ... Pick out those you like. Cross out those you find irrelevant. Identify what you are going to work on.

You gain strength, courage and confidence by every experience in which you really stop to look fear in the face. You must do the thing you think you cannot do.

(Eleanor Roosevelt)

Leadership in today's world requires far more than a large stock of gunboats and a hard fist at the conference table.

(Hubert H. Humphrey)

The real leader has no need to lead – he is content to point the way.

(Henry Miller)

The leader leads, and the boss drives.

(Theodore Roosevelt)

There is no such thing as a perfect leader either in the past or present, in China or elsewhere. If there is one, he is only pretending, like a pig inserting scallions into its nose in an effort to look like an elephant.

(Liu Shao-ch'i)

The quality of leadership, more than any other single factor, determines the success or failure of an organization.

(Fred Fiedler & Martin Chemers)

There is no contest between the company that buys the grudging compliance of its workforce and the company that enjoys the enterprising participation of its employees.

(Ricardo Sempler)

The first responsibility of a leader is to define reality. The last is to say thank you.

(Max DePree)

A friend of mine characterizes leaders simply like this: 'Leaders don't inflict pain. They bear pain.'

(Max DePree)

I used to think that running an organization was equivalent to conducting a symphony orchestra. But I don't think that's quite it; it's more like jazz. There is more improvisation.

(Warren Bennis)

When the effective leader is finished with his work, the people say it happened naturally.

(Lao Tse)

Leadership is understanding people and involving them to help you do a job. That takes all of the good characteristics, like integrity, dedication of purpose, selflessness, knowledge, skill, implacability, as well as determination not to accept failure.

(Admiral Arleigh A. Burke)

A competent leader can get efficient service from poor troops, while on the contrary an incapable leader can demoralize the best of troops.

(General of the Armies John J. Pershing)

No man will make a great leader who wants to do it all himself, or to get all the credit for doing it.

(Andrew Carnegie)

And finally ...

The only real training for leadership is leadership.

(Anthony Jay)

I'm sure you have seen enough quotes now, but I just wanted to give you a few more in respect of one important aspect of leadership – humility. It might be that you don't agree that leaders should be humble, but I would have to differ with you on that.

humility and leadership

> I think humility is often misunderstood as being a weakness, the ability to understand that as a leader you are fallible and that at times your way of thinking may need to be on a different route is a true leadership strength and sadly lacking in many. (T McCloskey)

> Humility is only one hallmark of a good leader, the art of leadership is bringing out the best in yourself and others and knowing intuitively when it is the time to step up, step aside or step together to achieve the greater good. (Heather Palmer)

> If humility includes putting your hands up and admitting you've got it wrong sometimes, then yes, that a sign of a good leader ... but best not done too often! (Richard Crouch)

Although the above are generic quotes about leaders, female leaders often lead in a very different way. I recently attended an Enterprising Women conference in Florida. At that conference this was the list given to us of the characteristics of great female leaders – through the eyes of some of the business women in the enterprising women community:

- ❖ Leaders take an holistic view of their business. Incorporating aspects such as issues within society, their community, their values and vision, they set business within the context of everything rather than view it in isolation of other issues.
- ❖ They dream big dreams and set big goals.
- ❖ They are comfortable doing things never done before. They have courage.
- ❖ They are motivated by passion rather than profit.
- ❖ They create exceptional teams and align values and vision of team members with business values and vision.
- ❖ They recognise the importance of networks.
- ❖ They talk about setting priorities and always being present in the current priority.
- ❖ They recognise the importance of being a change agent for other women.

I laugh when I read this list again. I know many men who would suck in their cheeks and sweat at some of the items. Picture that! It makes for uncomfortable reading if you were brought up to believe that a single-minded focus on maximising profit is the be all and end all to business. No wonder men are anxious about the 'havoc' all the ambitious women around the world wanting to be promoted to boards of directors will wreak.

Its not havoc, though. It's just that it's time to stand up and be proud of knowing that there is a different way to achieve things. Leadership behaviours were set and established by men hundreds of years ago. Women had no say in how those behaviours were set and established because at that time women did not get involved in business. But now we are and now we have an opportunity to challenge what the accepted norms of leadership behaviours are and what skill sets are expected.

networking

I have touched on the topic of networking a few times already, but in this section I want to talk about it in more detail as it is such an important activity when you set up and run your business.

When I was in education several decades ago no-one talked about the need for personal networks. That would have meant nothing to me. I am not a natural networker at all. In fact I am one of those in my private life who prefers a few genuine and sincere friends to whole hordes of contacts.

But in business, in today's environment, I'm afraid there is no choice. We all need wide networks of good quality contacts. So if you haven't already started, what you now need is a plan of how you are going to begin to build your network.

When starting out I spent hours and hours networking in groups and at meetings that actually generated very few of the right contacts either for business sales or for my personal support. I had a tendency to try and attend every networking opportunity in the vain hope that the number of hours invested would one day reap their reward. In hindsight I would do it very differently though. You have to be wise with your time – always.

It took me twelve years of being in business before I decided to join a female-only networking group. Prior to that I had stubbornly held onto the belief that we operate in a mixed-sex business world so mixed-sex networking was appropriate and right. For me, though, my networking only really began once I joined my first female-only networking group. Perhaps I personally just struggle to get taken seriously by men so networking in mixed-sex groups always just felt like banging my head against a brick wall. There are only so many times someone can assume you have come with your boss to fetch and carry his drinks before you decide enough is enough. I don't even look like a dolly bird for someone's arm, but people still assumed I was – just because I was a woman.

I wonder if I ought to make a confession here. There is a woman who has regularly invited me to link in with her on LinkedIn. I reject very few invitations if they come from people who I think would be a valuable contact. But I reject her. She will not remember, but many years ago I approached her at a networking function with a view to asking her if she would become my accountant as I wanted to change the firm I was using. However, she never broke off her conversation with the man she was talking to, even though I had made it clear I wanted to speak with her. And when eventually he left, she then brushed me off, saying she would love to talk but there was someone else she needed to see.

I knew there and then that she assumed I was some underling attending the networking lunch with my boss. I knew from her behaviour that she had written me off as someone not valuable to her network. I get frustrated when men make these assumptions, but I feel more than ticked off when women do the same. To this day she still though doesn't know why I won't accept her invite on LinkedIn!

One thing I recently learned about networking is that women and men approach it very differently. Men develop networks from a very young age with the full intention of using those networks as they progress through their careers and business life.

Women however, whilst they have friendships, do not create networks in the same way.

When women network in business, they often do so to build relationships, seek moral support, guidance and advice from other women. In contrast, when men network in business they seek sales leads and contacts from other men. No wonder men at networking functions quickly move on from some of the women they meet. We are networking for totally different reasons.

To overcome this difference, my suggestion is that you create two different types of network – those that will provide you with the support and friendship you are seeking, and those that will provide you with the sales leads and contacts that can be so valuable. I don't often choose to follow the men's lead, but on this I think learning how to network like men might help us all.

Once you have begun, developing your network is pretty critical. You can recruit your employees from your network, tap into known suppliers through it, get business information and advice, and of course get your customers or clients. You need to start building your network from day one in business.

If you are thinking of trading internationally at some point and are interested in some international networks, these are just three of the networks I currently belong to:

United Succes

UnitedSucces is a fabulous and inspirational organisation. It is a social enterprise that was established in 2008 by Corinne Heijn and is based in the Netherlands.

It is a 'by-invitation only' global organisation for women entrepreneurs who don't only want to succeed in business, but who are passionate about wanting to make a difference in the world.

UnitedSucces connects women around the world and in 2013 held its first annual symposium in Amsterdam for many of its members to meet each other and develop great relationships. Next year its members will meet in Nairobi to continue building relationships.

With offices in the Netherlands, New York and South Africa, and representatives in ten other countries (Canada, USA, UK, Hong Kong, Japan, Philippines, Brazil, Egypt, Uganda and Ghana), the UnitedSucces community is growing fast and its members operate across a broad range of industries in fifty-five countries, almost half of which are in emerging markets. UnitedSucces plans to grow the community to 4,000 female entrepreneurs across 150 countries by 2018.

The UnitedSucces Mission: economically empowered women, who have a support system they can depend on, have a significant impact on society, through investing in improved livelihood, health and education of their families and broader communities. By supporting the needs of emerging and established female entrepreneurs, and by sharing best practices of impactful and sustainable female-owned businesses, UnitedSucces aims to empower and support future responsible female leaders assisting them to make a lasting contribution to the communities and countries they operate in.

The Women President's Organization

The WPO has a membership of more than 1,600 women entrepreneurs across five continents. To become a member you need to be grossing $2 million in annual sales or $1 million if you are a service-based business.

A few facts and figures about its 1600 members provided very generously to me for this book by Marsha Firestone, Founder and President of the WPO:

- Average Revenue of businesses: $13 Million
- Aggregate Revenue of all members businesses: $18 Billion
- Average Years in Business: 23
- Aggregate Years in Business: 33,000 years!!
- Average Number of Employees: 93
- Aggregate Number of Employees: 135,000
- 70 % of WPO members do business with each other and/or WPO Corporate Sponsors.

- 11.5 % of members pay themselves a salary of more than $300,000 a year.
- 60% of members say the WPO has contributed to their economic success.

Once a year I meet around 750 WPO members at a three-day conference that is full of speakers and networking, but for me the greatest benefit of membership is in the monthly meetings I attend. Each month I meet with around fifteen WPO members who have over time become really valued contacts, advisors and supporters. One of the great things is that the recruitment process into WPO chapters dictates that the members of each group have to be in non-competing businesses, so each month we share information and challenges relevant to our businesses and provide each other with support.

WEConnect International

WEConnect International is a corporate-led not-for-profit organisation that facilitates inclusive and sustainable economic growth.

It achieves this by empowering and connecting women business owners globally. In just the few years that I have known them, the organisation has expanded enormously around the globe and is regularly entering new territories.

WEConnect connects women business owners to its corporate members that collectively represent over US$700 billion in annual purchasing power and include some of the most well known names around the world.

Any woman can apply to join as long as she owns 51% or more of her business.

There are many networking groups out there and with every passing year more and more of them are focused on networking for women. But do your research and choose carefully. If you are already a member of a women-only networking group but aren't sure if it is going to benefit you, here are three questions to ask yourself:

1. Do the women in the group think 'big' or 'small'? And, if the collective group thinking is 'small' is that going to stretch me?
2. Its nice to meet these same women once or twice, but if I meet them thirty times how will that enhance my knowledge, skills or sales leads?
3. Is there a level of honesty and integrity in the group that will enable me to share business information and seek support?

learning to say 'no'

I am pretty sure that you wouldn't find a chapter like this in a book for men setting up in business, but I find it is a failing of many of us women that we do not say 'no' when in fact we really want to, or ought to, say 'no'. Often it's because we want to be able to do what the other person asks, or we don't want to let them down, or we want to preserve the relationship. But not saying 'no' when we really ought to probably suggests that we have a few assertiveness skills to learn!

Can you think of a few occasions when you have said 'yes' or 'maybe' when in fact you should have said 'no'?

This is not just a small problem for women; for many it's a simply enormous issue. I have seen someone get married to a guy she didn't want to marry because he decided they were going to be married and she never found the courage to put him straight. I have seen endless women accept second dates from men they really didn't like just because they didn't know how to say no politely and be heard saying no. I have also seen women accept promotions and take on jobs at work that they really didn't want just because they couldn't work out how to say no and preserve the working relationship.

> I had to laugh at myself the other week as a potential client phoned and asked me if I would speak on diversity and inclusion at a conference they were running. There were two reasons I wanted to say 'no':
>
> ❖ I thought it was a company/group of people who were only interested in paying lip service to diversity and inclusion;
>
> ❖ I already had commitments that day.
>
> But I did what is so typical of me, I said 'yes' when in fact I meant 'no'. But then to wriggle out of the hole I had just dug for myself I then sent a quote over that I thought was so high they would turn around and say that I was too expensive!

> The last laugh was on them, though, as they then said 'yes', so I had to go and speak in a place I didn't want to and cancel something I had been really looking forward to.
>
> Oh! If only I practised what I preached and found the confidence more often to just say 'no'!

If you get an enquiry from a customer to provide a certain product or service that isn't in your current offerings, do you say 'no' or 'yes'?
For the most part you should probably say 'no' – unless your business is of a size that you have both time and resources to diversity your offering.

It is so easy to lose focus in business if you allow yourself to be continually led astray out of a desire to ease cash flow or please others by agreeing to everything offered. Continually diversifying your offering or product range can occasionally be a good thing, but it can be very distracting too so be careful you don't spend more time branching out than focusing on your core business.

The reality is that you only have so many hours in the day and a finite amount of energy. You therefore need to look after both carefully and always keep focused.

Sometimes others have a great idea for your business. They can be very persuasive. But no one knows your business as well as you do so always put them off and tell them you will consider their idea when you have time. If you're still hesitating, ask them what profit margin is in it, what the set-up costs will be, what it will take to bring it to market. And if they have answers to those three questions and are still pushing you after that, perhaps they are someone worth working with!

Whilst I urge you not to dabble in everything that might come your way, I was urged by my first ever client to provide a service he wanted and saying 'yes' to that was one of the best things I ever did in the early days of my business.

In the early days of my first business, I provided an employment law and employee relations advice service to small and medium-sized enterprises (SMEs). For the most part it was a telephone and email service and occasionally I met my clients face to face. At the time, though, I didn't like doing anything face to face, so it was relatively rare that I ventured out of my home office.

But one day a client phoned and said he wanted me to deliver training to his line managers as he had noticed that month after month he was paying me to sort out problems caused by line managers who were month after month, continually making the same mistakes when managing their staff.

I initially said 'no', to which he replied that if I wanted his business in the future then I needed to deliver the service he wanted from me and he wasn't going to take no for an answer!

Inevitably, given my endless desire to please and inability to say 'no', I agreed and went and delivered my first ever training course. Nervous does not begin to describe how I felt but I delivered a great course and from that day to this, training has been a core offering of my business. With time also, my confidence as a trainer has grown as has my confidence in working with people in business face to face. He has no idea what he did for both me personally and my business but that is one client I am so glad I said 'yes' to.

In fact he is still a client today – some seventeen years after first setting up.

learning to say 'yes'

You have to laugh, but the opposite problem of being able to say 'no' is learning to say 'yes' or 'thank you', which some women find equally difficult. You wouldn't believe we are the gender that has a reputation for non-stop talk!

I once sat in a sales meeting and heard a colleague four times not accept that the client wanted to buy. The incredible irony of the situation was that it was a global sales development training company that wanted to buy our HR services and she was trying to talk them down from buying! She kept offering alternatives in order to minimise their spend! But sometimes in business – and life – you need to learn to just say 'yes' and then shut up.

It's the same when someone says you've got a great business. How many women simply say 'thank you' compared to the number of women who smile but say 'oh I'm working on it', or 'for the most part we get it right', or 'one day it will be as I want it'?

Why can't we just say 'yes' or 'thank you'? We appear to have this constant desire to deliver even more than is expected, or please even more than we have already done, or not appear to have too much ego just in case someone finds that arrogant. I understand why it happens, but not just saying 'yes' or 'thank you' holds women back in business.

let me tell you a story ...

I regularly volunteer in schools helping students put together CVs, work on their interview skills etc. Often these children are about sixteen and ready to take on their first part time job as they continue to study. A few years ago, I did a mock interview with a girl who had submitted a one-page CV that showed she was a top academic performer and great musician as well.

When we shook hands she gave me a dainty little bob and tiny nod of her head that had a distinct oriental feel to it. She was, though, clearly of white UK ethnic origin and later explained that her mum was a teacher and her dad was a policeman, both working in a rural English village nearby.

My first question to her was about her strengths. In reply she said, 'I knew you were going to ask that, but I don't really have any.' Holding onto my patience I said that I was sure she did and to take a few moments to think before saying what they were. But a few moments passed and she repeated that she didn't really have any.

It can be hard work sometimes doing mock interviews with sixteen-year-olds who don't have any work experience yet, but I'm well practised so next I scanned her CV. It was all in font size 11 but there was a line at the bottom of the page that was probably in font size 6. It was a line about her interests. It said 'reading, cooking, going to the cinema, music, Japanese'. The first few are interests written on every schoolgirl's CV I have ever seen, but Japanese was unusual so I asked her about it and this is what (with considerable prompting) she said:

'When I was six I told my parents I wanted to learn Japanese. They thought I was being ridiculous but I kept on repeating it and eventually they bought me a 'teach yourself Japanese' book. So when I was six I started teaching myself Japanese and now I can speak it and write it and since I was twelve I also go by train to London (about a one-and-a-half-hour trip) on my own each Saturday and sing in a Japanese choir. My parents think I'm mad! I also want to go to Japan so a month ago I applied to do a year placement with a Japanese college. I'm really disappointed, though, as they have just turned me down as I am one week too old to apply for the placement course. I'm not giving up, though, and yesterday I sneaked out of school at lunchtime and phoned the college on my mobile to try to persuade them to change their mind. They said they will let me know in a few days' time.'

I then smiled and asked her, given this story, what she thought her strengths were. She looked blankly at me and said, 'I don't think I really have any, but I can tell you about my weaknesses.'

What on earth can you say in response to that?

And whilst this slight, dainty, head-bobbing girl remains in my thoughts, I remind myself why I am writing this book and why I want so many more women to find the courage to go out there and set up in business, or do whatever it takes so that they can hold their head up in society and say, 'I'm great at what I do and I have fantastic strengths that bring so much value to the work I do.'

woman or man?

I know that this section will be contentious with many but I think it's really important to address this issue right at the start of your business journey.

So many of us just drift into the roles we play in life or morph our behaviours little by little to best fit the environment we are in, but I want you to think about who you want to be in life (and in business).

Right from the start I felt that it was important for me to continue to act and behave like a woman in business. No compromises.

I did not want to:

- dress in man suits;
- tone down my make up so it would not offend (or scare) any man at any point;
- write the short blunt emails that so many men write that to me lack so much courtesy;
- take voice coaching to learn how to lower my voice just because someone said that would give me more 'gravitas';
- only wear grey or black so I never stood out or looked too (scarily) feminine;
- never openly challenge a man or back him into a corner by asking 'why' (I still don't get why you can't ask a man 'why' when all you want to know is 'why'. For goodness sake what are you supposed to ask 'who' or 'which'? Well that won't get you the answers you need!);
- justify why I wanted to spend so much working time doing voluntary work rather than maximising my profit;
- bone up on football and cricket so I could network with the men and pretend I liked what they liked just to be able to build a business relationship with them;
- pretend that I did not have children or childcare responsibilities or had to get home to cook the dinner;

- ❖ lie about the fact that I couldn't attend a networking breakfast as at that time of day I would be changing nappies or doing a school run;
- ❖ spend five hours every evening in the gym (instead of enjoying being with my kids or having some time for me) in some vain attempt to keep the body of a twenty-one-year-old who had never been pregnant just because some business guys like to be around women who look hot.

I'm exaggerating, of course, and compromise at times is important. But my observation over the years is that just too much compromise has been expected of women and equally, too much compromise has been made by women to the point at which many women in business are not really women at all – somehow over time they lost their own personality and natural style and developed into mini men. I am not quite sure the title 'mini man' fits with her, but one of the most obvious cases of this to me was Margaret Thatcher. She might have felt she had no choice but to adopt male behavioural and leadership traits, but to me she sold out.

You have to find what is right for you. Some women seem to enjoy being one of the 'boys', behaving and thinking like men in business, loving the cut and thrust and constant competition, and if that suits them (or you), then that is fine. But with more women entering into business, it's important that we do not all feel we have to lose our femininity and our sense of who we really are, in order to fit in and find acceptance.

In recruiting staff over the years, I have also actively avoided recruiting those who want me to act and behave like the women we so often see in the corporate world. Many of these women don't even realise what they have compromised over the years, so good has been the indoctrination in the corporate workplace. Even if you challenge them, these women will trot out all the traditional leadership competencies and behaviours that effectively bar them from the top jobs. Can't they see that?

It can be like talking to robots trying to get corporate women to question the accepted norms of behaviour in big business. Find me one who doesn't think that 'gravitas' is an essential trait of a leader. Then try to find me even one women who would be considered to have 'gravitas' who doesn't wear man suits and attend weekly coaching sessions to lower the tone of her voice.

I try to recruit people who will accept me for who I am, rather than endlessly criticise me for not conforming to social norms of business women operating in a man's business world.

But just because I want to stay true to my feminine self, that doesn't mean you should feel the same. Every one of us has to do what we feel is right for us. But what I want in this section is to get you to think about who you are as a person and how you want to behave in this enterprise you are creating without feeling a need to behave and think like a man just because others do. Take the time to make a conscious decision about how you are going to present yourself, rather than feeling you have drifted into – or been forced into – something a few years down the line.

> Its funny now, but it wasn't at the time ... I once had an employee make a complaint against me. She said that I lacked leadership skills as I had never shouted at her. Is this what employees expect? That I get aggressive and shout and stamp my foot when things don't go right? Tough, I am proud of the leadership skills I have and I feel no need to change my style to what might be considered a more masculine style just because someone thinks that's what all leaders should do.

who's threatened?

This might seem like an odd section, but I've decided to take the bull by the horns and address an issue that affects many. If nothing and no-one is threatened by you, then please skip this bit. My ideas here will only be relevant to some. This section has two halves ... because I always love simplicity and plain speaking, I have divided it up into 'men threats' and 'women threats'!

when men feel threatened

Let me start by saying that not all men feel threatened by women having careers. But some do and this section is about them.

I once knew a lovely lady. She was the mildest and meekest, but also kindest and most gentle-hearted soul you might ever meet. She cared for her four children and cooked and cleaned with endless grace. But one day, she announced to her family and friends that to bring in a bit more cash to the home and to give herself a bit of job satisfaction, she was going to start an ironing service. She would fetch washing from clients and bring it home to iron. At other times she would go and iron in other people's houses.

So her business wasn't going to set the world alight, but for so many women this is where they start their entrepreneurship journey. Something small and achievable that fits in with their other responsibilities. I don't know if you are aware, but 74% of all entrepreneurs in the UK are sole traders, so this lady was about to join the millions of others who thrive on working from home.

But then next time I saw her, her fledgling business had been closed. Why? In a nutshell, some men don't like their wives, partners or girlfriends working – working outside the home that is. Working out what drives their 'dislike', though, can sometimes be difficult.

Having talked to many women over the years, including spending time with women who used to work but now no longer do so, and time with women who are tiptoeing through precarious home lives, I would summarise the typical issues as men worrying that:

- others will think/comment on the fact they can't bring enough money home themselves;
- their wives are meeting people they know nothing about and whether their wife might be tempted to stray by any of these unknown men;
- this tiny enterprise might lead to something that might challenge their position in the family or society;
- their wife/partner will morph into some ambitious dragon woman that breathes fire;
- others in society might view their wife/partner as having ideas above her station and ultimately that might affect the stability of the marriage or the family.

Whatever the reason, I know of numerous women who have had to explain and justify their business and I know of significant numbers of women who haven't been allowed by their husband or partner to open their doors for business at all.

Society might not like to discuss or acknowledge the control and possessiveness issues that go on behind so many closed doors but they are there, so today I write about them. But I do so not to create dissent, but more to ensure that when you set up your business, you do so with your eyes open and have a good understanding of some of the issues you may have to deal with.

If you are one of the women affected by this, then you need to think very carefully before setting up in business. It is hard enough setting up anyway, but trying to run a business against a backdrop of hostility is an enormous task.

Equally, is this business worth endangering a stable relationship over? It might feel unfair that you don't have the freedoms that men have or that many other women have, but all of us need to deal with the life we have ... however unfair that may seem at times.

I am not saying, though, that just because you face hostility or difficulties you shelve your business plan; merely that you think carefully before proceeding. Perhaps starting very low-key is a viable alternative and only beginning to grow your business once your family has become adjusted to the idea. If you do this, you might find it helpful to work out who could champion you in this venture.

Whatever approach you decide to take, you must not feel alone. This happens to many women, so find some support and never feel alone.

As well as those things that can worry the male members of our families, other triggers for men feeling threatened by a woman in business include:

- Her salary or hourly rate is higher than his.
- Her hours of work impact on her availability at home to maintain the home.
- Her self-esteem and confidence increases which makes him uncertain of the relationship.
- She travels to places he does not and meets men he does not know.
- She becomes financially independent.
- She announces that her career will come before starting a family.
- She chooses a job or business that causes him social embarrassment.

when woman feel threatened

Moving on, the issue of women feeling threatened by women is of equal importance. I have seen throughout my career successful women kicking out the career ladder beneath them and raising the bar so high that other women have little chance of following them to the dizzy heights of the board table. I have also experienced women in low-level jobs or with no job at all undermining and criticising those of us who have careers. Not all women, of course, just enough women to make an impact!

A wise Irishman once talked to me about why women so often do not support change. I think the assumption I had made until that point was that women get jealous of successful women, particularly when it is evident that their own lives revolve around children and the house. But my wise Irishman reminded me that throughout time women have always taken responsibility for maintaining the traditions in society and ensuring stability. Whilst men have gone off 'hunting', women have stayed behind to tend the land, keep the house in order, raise the children and maintain traditions in the local community.

We see this practice of women maintaining traditions in their communities right across the world, from village festivities to religious celebrations. So what happens when a woman like me comes along and messes up the established order by setting up a business and booking flights so I can travel the world? It was always bound to ruffle feathers – of both men and women!

Interestingly, research has shown that only 4% of female business owners say that their main champion is a woman. I find this astonishing, but perhaps I have spent years being far too naïve about expecting other women to support not just me, but other women in business. It's great to hear, though, that so many women feel that they have a man encouraging them to succeed.

unconscious bias

I haven't really talked directly in this book about diversity issues in society. Although so much of what I have talked about, touches on the topic.

When my business first started delivering diversity training in companies twelve or more years ago, typically the agenda covered discrimination law such as sex discrimination and race discrimination.
Over time, though, the agenda morphed away from just discussing what the law required into discussing much more how our behaviours and actions could unwittingly cause breaches of discrimination law. You might think of this as indirect rather than direct discrimination.

But in recent years we have again morphed the agenda and now training focusses more on perceived fairness, how to make people feel included at work and raising awareness about how we all have unconscious biases and how these can impact at work.

More recently still I see people starting to use terminology like 'gender intelligence' and no doubt we will see more training in this area in the coming years.

If you are interested in a quick and easy study of gender intelligence that gives some great insight into how to work with and communicate with the opposite sex at work then you might want to read a book that has just recently come out called Work with Me by Annis and Gray.

* scan me

If you are interested in learning more about unconscious bias then, as an introduction to the topic, why not take a look at this fascinating infographic that my business Jaluch recently developed.

If you don't yet have a scanning app on your mobile phone then the infographic is available to see in the research tab on the Jaluch website (www.jaluch.co.uk).

But when thinking about unconscious bias in relation to men and women, remember that we all have biases – it is not just men with unconscious biases about the intelligence, value and strengths of women, but also women with unconscious biases about men in equal measure! There is learning for all of us in this field.

I remember one particularly telling story that relates to how powerful some of our biases can be, and whilst this story is about one black man's view of black men, I have no doubt that there could be similar stories about one woman's view of women in business. The story is that the widely respected black leader Jesse Jackson, is said to have admitted with a degree of embarrassment that if he was out walking at night and heard footsteps behind him, he would nervously look back, but then feel relief if he saw the person walking behind him was white. It is simply incredible that our conditioning about different groups within our societies can make us biased against the group that we ourselves belong to. I am sure, though, that there are whole books written on the topic of conditioning, so please go and have a read if this interests you.

But returning to the topic of unconscious bias in how it relates to women setting up in business, some of the reading I have done and research I have come across reveals many things including:

- ❖ Both men and women have a tendency to value women's skills less than men's skills. In practical terms this means that you might at times struggle to get people to buy from you at the hourly rate or day rate that they would buy from a man. I have often urged self-employed women to up their charge-out rate as many of us have a tendency to ask for significantly less than men, but if you do so, be aware of this unconscious bias as it could mean that by asking for an amount equal to that which a man would ask, you could lose the sale.
- ❖ Both men and women have a tendency to view women as homemakers rather than breadwinners, which if you are pitching for business could impact on their confidence in you to deliver on a large project.

- Women can also be viewed as taking fewer risks in business (and life generally), therefore an organisation that is a high risk taker may not want you to work with them for fear of you seeking to reign in their risk taking or even whistleblow if what they are doing has crossed the line at all.
- Women are judged far more harshly than men in the business environment if they are overweight or underdressed (i.e. not looking glam enough or alternatively, have too much flesh showing!). Women are often judged more on their appearance than on what comes out of their mouths or minds. In my view, women judge women on appearance, just as much as men judge women.

making a difference and giving back to others

The final section of this chapter looks at making a difference and giving back. If you are thinking of setting up in business with a view to giving back to society or making a difference, then you will be amongst many.

Setting up a charity or social enterprise is very common for women. However, from watching a number of charities and social enterprises across the years here are a few learning points:

- Cash flow is king (perhaps given that this section follows on from unconscious bias I ought to have said cash flow is queen!) and if you are so generous with your funds wanting to support others that you go bankrupt due to not managing your cash flow then you won't have much to offer others. So don't be so generous that you put your business common sense to one side.

- Staff can be the greatest cost of any business, and long-term success can often be down to a business successfully managing its costs. Therefore you need to be careful who you employ and how much they cost. Do not let your desire to provide work for others damage your long-term prospects or ability to ever break even.

- I once heard someone say that even charities need to make a profit. This is good advice as you are aiming each year for break even, but if you make a loss you will probably go bust. So you need to aim each year for just a small profit. So set your social enterprise up with this in mind and do not become one of those who say that profit is a dirty word. Profit is not a dirty word, instead it is what will keep your social enterprise – and your dreams and passions – afloat in the coming year.

- In respect of employment law, in most countries there are no allowances made for charities or social enterprises. The same goes with accounting and many other business legalities. Therefore, please don't make the mistake that the set-up structure and processes within a charity or social enterprise can be informal and relaxed. They cannot, and if anything, you might come under even greater scrutiny.

Over the years, what I have also seen is women setting up a profit-making business, but then through that business, putting a lot of time and effort into 'giving back'. I personally try to spend around 10% of my time on my voluntary activities (which often involve working in schools, sharing my knowledge, mentoring and coaching and public speaking etc.). Be careful, though, as you still need to earn your bread and butter, so only put time into giving back, once your business is established enough to be able to support you doing that. I find it really hard to say 'no' sometimes when people ask me for favours and for my time, but sometimes you need to be as disciplined with saying 'no' as you are with running your business.

I can't preach here as I am well known for not being able to say 'no' and ending up with huge diary commitments as a result. Ultimately this is not a good position to be in, though, and I recognise that!

And finally, whilst giving back may be important to you, you might be interested to know that its becoming more and more important to employees too. So if you work within your community, don't keep this a secret or keep it so low-key that no-one is aware. You might feel bashful about it, but you will attract in and retain staff with similar values to your own if you open up about your community and other voluntary activities. It is after all, something we should be really proud of.

CHAPTER ELEVEN

so are you going for it?

I have given you so much information your head may well be swimming with it all. I hope I haven't overloaded you. What I have tried to do is give you an insight into the many different areas of business and some of the challenges you may face. I hope I have given you ideas too of how to set up and how to run your fledgling company. But now you need to decide if you are actually going to go ahead with it, and create the enterprise you have been dreaming about.

Whilst this book is called My Business, My Success when choosing a title I conducted an online poll and one title came out as a firm favourite. That title was From Dream to Reality. Clearly women have been dreaming about business and would love the opportunity to stop dreaming and start doing. Unfortunately we couldn't use that title as it was already taken, but what I have written here in this book is with a view to helping you turn your dreams into reality.

But enough from me ... and its over to you – decision time!

reasons why you really shouldn't launch right now

As you have dipped in and out of this book I have no doubt that you have spent more time thinking about the reasons you might fail than thinking about the joy and excitement you will feel should you, by some miracle, succeed!

Personally, I think you should sort your head out and just launch(!). However, here is my (slightly) more sensible list of why you are right and you really shouldn't launch right now:

- ❖ There are fears you have that you cannot yet, or do not yet know how to, overcome.
- ❖ You haven't yet found a way to sensibly manage your own stress levels.
- ❖ It's comforting listening to the doubters and believing them.
- ❖ You quite like not believing in yourself as it gives you a great safety zone.
- ❖ You still can't shift your thinking away from believing that all needs to be perfect before you launch and that somehow at some point there will be a perfect time to launch and you are just happy waiting for it.
- ❖ You are too busy thinking up reasons why you shouldn't launch to do any sensible business planning and I have to admit that I did set out in earlier chapters that you really shouldn't launch without a business plan!
- ❖ You are still listening to the confidence vampires and society dragons who like to keep you under control, so you persist in your belief that you can't combine motherhood and owning your own business.
- ❖ You haven't yet worked out that your kids will always love you if you love them, and that they will probably be pretty proud if their mother is a successful business owner – even if that means not always being there for them when they come out of school.
- ❖ You are just plain scared and don't know who to talk to about that!

But let's not leave it there ...

reasons why you really should launch RIGHT NOW

As many who know me well will confirm, patience is not my strongest virtue! For my part I really don't know why you didn't launch first and then buy this book second to do some reading about how to get it right!

An interesting woman I talked to recently told me about a survey of people who had resigned their roles in large companies. They discovered during this research that men first thought about leaving around six months before they actually left, and usually they left because they had a new job to go to. In contrast, women first thought about leaving around two years before they actually went, and at the point of going they had not yet got around to looking for or finding an alternative role, but instead left due to a 'last straw' moment. Personally, I think too many women spend too much time thinking about 'what if' or 'should I', so I think every single one of you should aim to launch RIGHT NOW!

But here are some other more sensible reasons that have nothing (or at least not very much) to do with my impatience:

- ❖ The economy needs more female entrepreneurs – we run more robust businesses, go bust less often, employ more people, innovate more, rely on risky external financing less and the list goes on and on.
- ❖ Inaction achieves nothing and changes nothing. For me action is all important.
- ❖ It's probably time to stop making excuses and delaying.
- ❖ Leadership is not about following others, it is about leading the way and to do that you have to take action.
- ❖ Is the world ever going to change if you delay?
- ❖ 'Don't put off till tomorrow something that you can do today.'
- ❖ Other women are waiting to look up to you and see you show the world that it can be done.

- If the one million female entrepreneurs in the UK all employed just one more person, then the problem of unemployment in the UK would cease to exist, and the same applies to many economies in the world. You need to believe that your contribution matters.

- This is the first step towards your financial independence, so why are you holding back? Do this for yourself and for your family, and remember that financial independence is the way to ensure that you have choices in life. Without money your choices can be very limited.

- This is a first real step towards you being able to give back to your community – female entrepreneurs put around 80% of what they earn back into their communities, whilst men only put back around 35-40%. How amazing will it be if you can put back so much into your community?

- This is your first step to creating a world that is truly fit for all of our daughters.

- I really want you to come and join me on what is probably going to be the most thrilling ride we are ever likely to go on in our lifetime – it may be a roller-coaster, but it's our roller-coaster!

CHAPTER TWELVE

advice, guidance & inspiration from the best!

In this chapter I want to inspire you; to make you think, to give you an opportunity to avoid all the mistakes everyone else has made, and an opportunity to learn from some fantastic role models from around the world whom I am lucky enough to have either met or have in my network.

Each and every one of these women has given their precious time in answering my questions because they believe passionately in supporting other women to set up and run their businesses.

I would particularly like to thank Tina Thomson and the rest of the fantastic UnitedSucces team for helping gather so many women together to give us their ideas.

Elaine Strydom
Africa Transport Holdings (Pty) Ltd (South Africa)

Website: www.movit.co.za

Age when first set up: 41

Main product or service: Road, sea and air freight. This includes moving household effects, office equipment, aircraft, yachts and even a dismantled diamond mine to Armenia.

Staff numbers: 10-50 staff.

One mistake made in early years: Not bringing an accountant on board from inception.

One real strength that you bring to business: Networking and organisational skills.

Main challenge in business: Being a woman in a man's world.

Advice for other entrepreneurs: Turnover is vanity, profit is sanity and cash is reality.

Personal motto in business: Leadership is not about having everyone agree with you, it is about taking responsibility. Also it's not what has gone wrong, it's about how I fix it!!!!!!!!! Also: You are never too old to dream, never too old to have goals.

Anything else? And ... Winston Churchill said: You never, never, never, never ever give up!!

Alicia B. Carballo
Alicia Carballo & Asocs
(Argentina)

Website: www.carballohr.com

Main product or service: Executive search, outplacement and coaching.

Staff numbers: Two plus many freelance professionals.

One mistake made in early years: Worrying too much.

One real strength that you bring to business: My intuition and I like helping people progress. My strong leadership and commitment.

Advice for other entrepreneurs: Once you decide what you want, don't overthink it … Just do it.

Personal motto in business: I like people and I like being with people. Having empathy is good; it helps you gain a lot of experience of life and work. Ethics is also very important to me. That's why I have such nice friends and try to select good people for my clients.

Anything else? Fear is the enemy of action. Always try to improve the level of your work and be kind to people. Sometimes people in business try to get us to lower our fees. This can be a big temptation, but if this means you then deliver a lower level of work … in the end you will lose out. Reputation is difficult to get and easy to lose.

Julie Weeks
Womanable
(US-based but operate internationally)

Website: www.womenable.com

Age when first set up: 47

Main product or service: Service business consulting with the enablers of women's entrepreneurship to conduct research, improve policies and programmes, build NGP organisational capacity – all with the aim of improving the environment for women who are starting or growing businesses.

One mistake made in early years: Probably not being as strategic as I should have been in picking clients to pursue; the business grew organically very early on, but could have grown faster with more strategic intention.

One real strength that you bring to business: Knowledge of subject matter and the ability to translate complex information into actionable recommendations.

Main challenge in business: Proactively marketing myself and my firm's services.

Advice for other entrepreneurs: Don't be afraid to stumble or change direction; entrepreneurship is about creating something new and different, so there is no single best way to grow your business – you have to learn by doing, so just start doing it!

Personal motto in business: My motto, if you can call it that, is a quote that inspires me, from anthropologist Margaret Mead: 'Never doubt that a small group of thoughtful, committed citizens can change the world. Indeed, it's the only thing that ever has.'

Amanda Pelham Green
Odyssey Mentor Limited
(UK)

Website: www.odysseymentor.com

Age when first set up: 27

Main product or service: International relocation: home search, school search, cross-cultural training etc.

Staff numbers: 50, of whom 25 were freelance.

One mistake made in early years: Not planning the office space carefully enough for growth. We ended up moving offices four times in twelve years, which was an expensive and disruptive process.

One real strength that you bring to business: The rain maker/I'm a great networker.

Main challenge in business: Finance – I understand the big picture and can drill down if I have to, but would rather someone else were doing it; as long as I know it's ok I don't want to be bothered with the detail.

Advice for other entrepreneurs: Be clear about your vision, set realistic intentions, plan your exit (if you want one) way ahead of time.
Personal motto in business: Never be afraid to ask for advice; care for your network, handwritten thank you notes go a long way; dare to be different.

Madeleine van der Steege
SYNQUITY
(Netherlands)

Website: www.synquity.com

Age when first set up: 38

Main product or service: We sync people, teams and organisations through coaching and interactive research surveys.

One mistake made in early years: Doubting myself.

One real strength that you bring to the business: Courage/initiative.

Main challenge in business: Consistent networking is a challenge.

Advice for other entrepreneurs: It takes time, be patient/realistic BUT get working on everything at the same time – creating your product/brand + network+ build your team+ deliver the product or service+ administrate+ get internet and social media savvy+ use Apps!!

Personal motto in business: Be true to yourself and never stop learning. Live and work in a manner that you may have no regrets.

Anything else? Inclusivity and partnerships are very efficient ways of expanding your reach and bringing others on board.

Sarah Steel
The Old Station Nursery Group (UK)

Website: www.theoldstationnursery.co.uk

Age when first set up: 32

Main product or service: Childcare and consulting in the early years sector in UK and overseas.

Staff numbers: 200

Turnover last year: £3M

One mistake made in early years: Not outsourcing some of the tasks that kept me so busy – such as bookkeeping.

One real strength that you bring to business: Leadership has been vital in rolling out my vision across many sites which are also geographically spread.

Main challenge in business: Managing cash flow to allow rapid growth. Also getting new staff to buy into our company values when we acquire existing sites.

Advice for other entrepreneurs: You have to have self-belief – if you don't believe in yourself, no one else will!

Personal motto in business: Fortune favours the brave!

Robyn Heathfield

Torquip Earthmoving: Mining Equipment
(Southern Africa)
Neutral Futures Ltd: Forest Protection REDD
(Mauritius, Mozambique, Zimbabwe, West Africa)

Age when first set up: 19

Main product or service: Supply of mining equipment, mining trucks over 100T and sale of carbon credits generated by the protection of forests.

Staff numbers: 50+

One mistake made in early years: Too many to count, but a big one was not advertising and relying on word of mouth to build a customer base.
One real strength that you bring to business: Persistence and long-term vision.

Main challenge in business: Managing staff, admin and short-term organisation.

Advice for other entrepreneurs: Don't give up ... deviate, diversify, adapt, but don't give up.

Personal motto in business: Honesty always wins, tell one lie and you will never be able to tell the truth again.

Anything else? Unless you operate in a small niche market, good advertising and marketing is the differentiator between a slow-growing business and a fast-growing business.

Carrie Bedingfield
Onefish Twofish
(UK)

Website: www.onefishtwofish.co.uk

Age when first set up: 25 (but lots of small enterprises when younger).

Main product or service: Creative business communication – how to get the attention of people at work, whether they are potential clients or employees.

One mistake made in early years: I expected employees and partners to be the same as me – and I wasn't good at taking people with me. Inspiring clients was relatively easy, compared with inspiring my own team. I learnt over time to recognise and value people different from me and to try and engage on their terms, rather than mine.

One real strength that you bring to business: I think my strength is listening and thinking up/packaging interesting and creative ideas quickly.

Main challenge in business: Coaching. Though I REALLY want to be a safe place that people I work with can have their best ideas, I find myself in 'tell mode' far more often than I would like.

Advice for other entrepreneurs: Decouple yourself from the business. Otherwise you will have no choice but to ride the roller-coaster of client/employee/financial highs and lows. Not only is this exhausting but it keeps you small. You can't lead or be strategic if you're riding the roller-coaster. Your business is a game – one to take seriously, but one that is part skill (and this takes time to learn) and part luck. Business is something you do, not who you are. One way to do this is to have another focus outside of work. For me, this was sport (cycling competitively and then later marathon running). If things are tough in the business, making progress in this other area of my life brings a great deal of perspective.

Personal motto in business: Only spend your time on things that give joy in the doing or satisfaction in the having done. Otherwise, say no with grace (and glee!).

Anything else? You're the meanest boss you'll ever have. No one enjoys working for a mean boss for very long. So be a nice boss to yourself and you'll have a long, happy career.

Gill Thorpe
The Sourcing Team Ltd
(UK)

Website: www.sourcing.co.uk

Age when first set up: 32

Main product or service: Global sourcing & procurement specialised in promotional products.

Turnover last year: £1M+

One mistake made in the early years: Gave shares to the wrong person!! It cost lots to then buy out! Gave her too much too soon ...

One real strength that you bring to business: My strength is my diverse background, my procurement expertise and I'm great at finding opportunities.

Main challenge in business: Challenging staff/HR; finance sometimes.

Advice for other entrepreneurs: Build a brilliant support/expert network around you and give others support as well as asking for support.

Personal motto in business: Treat everyone with respect and in an ethical way – what goes around comes around! Care about everyone within or around your business.

Anything else? It's hard work, but it's so wonderfully rewarding too!!

Sherry Moran
TRiBECA® Knowledge
(UK)

Website: www.tribecaknowledge.com

Age when first set up: 20 (Tribeca Knowledge is my third business set up in 2002).

Main product or service: We are the global leader in innovative digital tools for pharmaceutical, biotec and medical device companies.

One mistake made in early years: I did all the work, kept all the profit, and didn't expand enough.

One real strength that you bring to business: Optimistic, fearless and innovative.

Main challenge in business: Networking, marketing.

Advice for other entrepreneurs: Identify your strengths and weaknesses and bring in someone to cover the weaknesses.

Personal motto in business: Stay in the present moment. That is where the opportunities are and they are not what you thought they would be. Plans are a good guide, but don't be too attached to them since life is fluid and will bring you more than you can ever imagine!!!

Anything else? Life balance is critical. Don't forget to enjoy the play of life without attachment

Karen Emanuel

Key Production Ltd
(London)
Think Tank Media, PIAS Production, Decadent Properties Ltd, Jicaro Island Ecolodge (Nicaragua)

Websites: www.keyproduction.co.uk
www.thinktankmedia.co.uk
www.jicarolodge.com

Age when first set up: 25

Main product or service: Various, including turning good ideas into great products and hospitality.

Staff numbers: 20 UK and 30 Nicaragua.

One mistake made in early years: Being honest and open.

One real strength that you bring to business: Being honest and open!

Main challenge in business: Managing staff.

Advice for other entrepreneurs: Be passionate, be patient, get a good accountant.

Personal motto in business: Never say never.

CHAPTER THIRTEEN

a little about me

And finally, I want to leave you with just a little about me – a little about what I've done, what I've seen and what I've learned ... which ultimately have all led to this book!

in the beginning

I am Helen Jamieson. Once I used to be Helen Parsons. I was young then and didn't know what I could do in life. At school I was a 'B'-grader. I didn't like school and they probably didn't like me much either. I was far too shy for anyone to think I would ever make anything of myself. I prided myself on my ability to fly under the radar! What an idiot!

At university I studied Arabic and, despite spending a year in Qatar part-way through my course as the first ever non-Muslim and non-Arab to have studied at the girls' university in Doha, I just scraped through to get an MA. For four years I was totally unmotivated and really disappointed by my uninspiring lecturers. I suppose in hindsight I didn't inspire them either! However, I managed to walk out of university and straight into a great graduate job with a nice big corporate working in their nice shiny offices in central London. So as luck and life would have it, I actually managed to start out on the right career ladder. But then I married and became Helen Clarke.

(Not all nationalities take on the surname of the husband, but most in the UK still do and that is what I did.)

At that point, you could say that I was somewhere between young and old, but I still didn't really know what I could do in life, or even what I wanted to do and I certainly didn't know what my strengths were. At twenty-nine years of age I started having children. Three of them. (Actually it was four as my first baby was stillborn, but I usually tell people I have had three as talking about stillborn children is still a bit of a social taboo – heaven forbid should we embarrass anyone!) I didn't have my three children all in one go of course! There is about five years between the eldest and the youngest. But as a result of creating this family, somehow my first name became 'mother' and my surname became synonymous with 'wife'. All good roles of course, but none of them were really about me, what I could do and what I could bring to the world.

But one thing changed around this time and it stemmed from my stillborn child. I have a lot to thank him for. I got to hold him, but I never really met him and I never got to see the colour of his eyes, but he taught me one really important thing. In the time leading up to his death, I worked really hard and had a two-hour round trip by car each day from the office. It was hard with my stomach getting bigger every day, but my boss said he didn't want me to go on maternity leave just yet as the office was too busy. I felt pressurised to hang on until the very last minute. I was also far too unassertive, hadn't even begun to learn to say 'no' and in my eagerness to please, I stayed working.

But around two weeks before my baby was due to be born, I had had enough. I was really tired and I could barely fit behind the steering wheel of my car. So one day I refused (by phoning in sick) to go to a business meeting that would have involved seven or eight hours driving in just one day. When my boss discovered that evening that I hadn't attended my meeting, he phoned me. He was angry and said that if that was my attitude to my job then he would be at my house next day to take away my company car. That night my baby died. Who knows if James died as a result of my stress? Perhaps he died because I wasn't assertive enough to give up work a week or so earlier?

We will never know whose fault it was or even if it was anyone's fault, but from that day onwards my motto became 'life is too short'. And from that little phrase stems so much of my current determination and focus.

Its funny, isn't it, how it's the tough stuff in life that can make us stronger.

I think I was a good wife and mother, but clearly something went wrong and I ended up getting divorced in my mid-forties. I then became Helen Jamieson. Legally, I didn't have to change my name after my divorce, but I wanted to. I wanted to become a person in my own right. Does that make any sense to you? So I changed my name by deed poll. I changed it to something that would forever enable me to remember my first stillborn baby who unwittingly gave me so much direction in life. And now I am Helen Jamieson, I know what I am about and I know what I want and I have my own identity which gives me so much satisfaction.

Years earlier, though, when I was still Helen Clarke and my oldest child was just two and my youngest child was just one, I set up in business. For me it wasn't really a matter of choice, more of necessity. I had become something of an embarrassment at work after losing my first baby following my boss having a temper tantrum, so my employer didn't really like me much. So, a year or so later, following the birth of my daughter and my return to work, they excluded me by giving me no work to do – for three long months. It was embarrassing. It was humiliating. And the damage to your self-esteem when you are treated like that is simply enormous.

But who wants to work somewhere they are unwanted? Not surprisingly, given my new motto of 'life is too short', I left.

a rookie in business

So with no job, young babies at home and a serious allergy to washing up and ironing (!) what does any woman with dreams do? She sets up her own business, of course. And after being made to feel she had no value with her last employer, she is now driven to deliver a service and find clients that recognise and reward her value. So that is what I did. And I did it alongside bringing up my gorgeous children.

My aim, inevitably, with young children at home, was to work part time. Unfortunately that is one part of my dream I have never really got sorted. Somewhere along the line I discovered that it takes a genius to be self-disciplined enough to stay part time when it is your own business.

And in terms of what my business did? Well, I did what many women do, I just took my existing skill set (human resources, employment law, employee relations) and set up as a self-employed consultant working from home. Not very imaginative, I know, but my dreams at that time extended as far as running my own business, not operating a business for which I felt I had no knowledge or experience to bring to the table. I know I could do that now, but I wasn't confident enough to do it then.

For five years I ran my HR consultancy. I worked from home, had another baby, built up a client base, delivered great service, developed my self-confidence, renewed my self-esteem, recruited my first employee and then, after five years, I was bought out.

It was a momentous day the day I sold my first business. I was in effect selling my 'baby'. My business had given me my self-confidence and my self-esteem and shown me that I could create something of value. I sold it on 9/11. The Twin Towers were crumbling and I was signing away my business.

I wanted a break, time to spend with my young children. My plan was to accept the director role offered to me by the large company that bought my business, work for them for a few weeks or months to assist the transfer and the resign so that I could spend time with the children.

That never happened, of course. In fact I have discovered in time that very little of what you plan for happens exactly the way you plan it to. It's another lesson, of course, for those setting up in business, go with the flow and prepare for the unexpected. So I stayed with that company for eleven months, running their HR consultancy and then, eleven months after arriving, they made an overnight decision to close it down.

Just one week later my second business was set up. I should have named it Phoenix as it was born out of the ashes of my last company, but Harry Potter wasn't that well known then and Phoenixes weren't at the forefront of my mind! So my second company came into being, identical to my first business, in fact, and with most of the same clients. But this time around we were a team of four, more knowledgeable, more experienced and this was effectively round two!

from a rookie to half way up everest

My second business has now been operating for well over ten years. It's been tough, but it's been an adventure and I now think we are half way up Everest. Just a few more metres to go!!

Our clients are spread right across the UK and we have really great staff. We know what we are doing and we know what we are selling, we know what our ideal customer looks like and we know how to stand up for ourselves. We innovate continuously, constantly strive to learn from our mistakes, and most importantly, we know we are infinitely better than so many of our competitors for a whole host of reasons.

I have also spent time over the past three years trying to expand my UK business into Saudi Arabia and the Gulf. I have networked with women around the world, been to places that I only dreamt about before and met countless people who inspired me and supported me.

Just two years ago, I was invited to become an EU female entrepreneurship ambassador. This is a voluntary role that provides me with fantastic opportunities to share my knowledge and experience with schoolchildren, students and business women. It's this sort of opportunity to work with and support others that motivates me day after day to get out of bed and do a great job. Being able to inspire and empower other women is such a phenomenal feeling and I hope no one ever takes that away from me.

And then, to end this part of my journey, in early 2013 I received in Florida an 'enterprising women of the year' award. But rather than inflate my ego, the reality is that that award has made me realise how little I have yet achieved, how very much more I want to do and how incredibly much there is to do to fly the flag for female entrepreneurship and to inspire and empower other women around the world. I would therefore love it – and be really honoured – if you would join me on this next part of my journey.

so, in a nutshell seventeen years ...

Seventeen years of unbelievable blood, sweat and tears, but also seventeen years of incredible satisfaction, enjoyment and sense of self-achievement.

Seventeen years of learning things the hard way, but also seventeen years of discovering endless new ideas.

Seventeen years of juggling more balls than the average toy box holds, but also seventeen years of achieving and doing more than I could ever have envisaged in one lifetime.

in conclusion

I don't really know where to start in concluding this book. I feel as though I have left out as much as I have included, which is very frustrating but I have to stop somewhere. But most of all, I am left with the distinct impression that in writing this book I have probably learned more than you will by actually reading it. I'm not sure that was the way it was meant to be!

Most notably I have learned:

- that I ought to stop and reflect even more often than I currently do;
- that throughout the past decade and a half it is not men, children or life that has held me back the most, but me and that silly irritating voice in my head that makes me doubt what I can do;
- that I still struggle to justify spending money on my own development and putting me first, even though I know that if I don't it will affect the business;
- that I still haven't learnt how to really say 'no' and be comfortable with that;
- that I have so much more to learn.

During the process of writing I have been able to look back on my journey and realise how very far I have come. I am actually pretty proud of myself for that! But I also realise that with so much more to learn and do, my journey is only just beginning.

please keep in touch

I wish you all the very best in your own travels, with all their twists and turns, and I would love it if you are able to share your adventures and ideas with others.

Visit the My Business, My Success website to share your thoughts and pick up new materials that I wasn't able to fit into this book. I will be regularly adding new material.

If you would like me to speak at a conference or seminar please do get in touch: helen@jaluch.co.uk.

If you would like to work with me to develop some female entrepreneurship workshops for your community, I would be thrilled to be involved, so do ask.

If you have questions, concerns, ideas or inspiration, please do use the email address above to get in touch.

I would also love it if you would:

- Link In with me: Helen Jamieson;
- Follow me on Twitter @HelenJamieson01 and @JaluchHelen;
- Join our **My business, My Success** LinkedIn group;
- Like us on Facebook too – www.facebook.com/mybusinessmysuccess

appendix: further reading

For those of you who want just a few more facts, figures, references and further reading (warning though that some of this is not for the faint hearted!):

One of my first comments in this book was ... 'This book is for those who want to help change the world for their daughters.' I am sure when some of you read this, it might have sounded a little trite. It was certainly not intended that way.

I hope that some of the following puts my interest in female entrepreneurship around the world in context.

Not so long ago, in an incredibly unsatisfactory phone conversation with a global diversity director, I was left with the distinct impression that she was of the opinion that if women really want to achieve seniority in business, they just need to work harder and longer, as success surely comes to all who those work hard. It saddens me and also horrifies me (and I don't use that word lightly) that this woman is not the only global diversity director I have come across in the past twelve months who actually does not have one clue about the issues relating to women in society and in the workplace. How on earth was she appointed to the role of global diversity director? These are the appointments made by corporates that have the power to change the world for women, but from what I have seen, so many appointments being made are given to the power-playing alpha females who do not actually appear interested in the women in the world. These women diminish the role for other global diversity directors who do take the role seriously.

As I have gone through life I have seen more, and learnt more, about women in the world than I ever thought possible. Women are living through things that are quite simply unimaginable to me. What I have come to realise, though, is that women who have achieved seniority in businesses need to educate themselves better about women's issues so that they can promote and facilitate change. Women should not be afraid to be threatened or called a 'feminazi' or to challenge men (and other women) on their behaviours.

We have to stand up for each other and we have to support each other if we are to achieve change.

For those of you who would like to be better informed about women around the world, perhaps some of the following information, articles and statistics will be of interest.

You might expect me to turn immediately to the Far or Middle East, but let's start instead with Italy:

An extract from an article by Barbie Latza Nadeau – October 22, 2012:

> In Italy, one woman is murdered every other day. Femicide in Italy has been increasing by around 10 percent a year for the past three years—faster than any other European country, according to Non Siamo Complici, or We Are Not Accomplices, a group that is working to empower women to stand up to domestic violence. Nearly 70 percent of the women were killed by men they lived with; most of the rest were killed by former boyfriends and ex-husbands; a tiny fraction were killed by their own sons or strangers. But it is not a manifestation of strength that is behind the growing number of casualties. It is a manifestation of weakness as men come to terms with a societal change in which women are finally rising to positions of power. Giorgia Serughetti, a doctor of cultural studies who helped form the women's empowerment group Se Non Ora Quando? (If Not Now When?) says some men fear that the women they once considered as possessions will feel empowered by seeing examples of strong women around them. 'This violence is because of the profound changes this country is going through regarding the roles of women in society,' Serughetti told Newsweek. 'It's because of women's liberation.'

Next up, lets look at China:

> In September 1997, the World Health Organization's Regional Committee for the Western Pacific issued a report claiming that 'more than 50 million women were estimated to be 'missing' in China because of the institutionalized killing and neglect of girls due to Beijing's population control program that limits parents to one child.' (See Joseph Farah, 'Cover-up of China's gender-cide', Western Journalism Center/ FreeRepublic, September 29, 1997.) Farah referred to the gendercide as 'the biggest single holocaust in human history'.

> I know that this extract is from 1997 but little has changed since then

in respect of the murder of baby girls around the world due to their perceived worth in society. Millions continue to be killed, particularly in China, India and the Middle East.

And moving on to Africa:
Huffington Post – July 2013

> A new U.N. report in July finds that nearly 100 million African girls and women have already undergone Female Genital Mutilation or Circumcision (FGM/C) and another 30 million are expected to endure the practice.
>
> While the percentage of girls being mutilated has fallen somewhat in recent years, the practice remains entrenched in ancient social patterns fueled by superstition.
>
> Despite years of pleading by Western and African health workers millions of families from Nigeria to Egypt are still about to put their children under the knife to cut off their clitoris and sometimes labia.
>
> The percentage of girls being cut is somewhat reduced in recent years in the 29 countries in Africa and the Middle East where female mutilation is practiced, said the report by UNICEF - the UN children's agency. On average 36% of girls ages 15-19 have been cut compared to an estimated 53% of women ages 45-49.
>
> But in places such as Egypt, cutting remains nearly universal.

And moving from Africa to the UK:

Despite what many women in the UK choose to believe, we need to take a look at the UK too. Here are some statistics from the Women's Aid website:

> Though only a minority of incidents of domestic violence are reported to the police, the police still receive one call about domestic violence for every minute in the UK, an estimated 1,300 calls each day or over 570,000 each year. (Stanko, 2000). However, according to the British Crime Survey, less than 40% of domestic violence crime is reported to the police (Dodd et al, July 2004; Walby and Allen, 2004; Home Office, 2002).

Repeat victimisation is common. 44% of victims of domestic violence are involved in more than one incident. No other type of crime has a rate of repeat victimisation as high (Dodd et al, July 2004).

Women assaulted by men they know: The self-completion module of the 2001 British Crime Survey research found that 'women are most commonly sexually assaulted by men they know'. When the researchers asked women about the last incident of rape experienced since the age of 16, they found that 45% were raped by current husbands or partners, 9% by former partners, and a further 29% of perpetrators were otherwise known to the victim. Only 17% were raped by strangers (Walby & Allen, 2004).

And finally, a few statistics take from the Women of the World website:

- Half the women in the world above age 15 cannot read or write.
- Worldwide, 62 million girls are not attending primary school.
- Violence causes more death and disability worldwide among women ages 15-44 than war, cancer, malaria, or traffic accidents.
- An estimated 50,000 women and children are trafficked into the United States annually for sexual exploitation or labour. Globally, 4 million women and girls are trafficked annually
- Close to 1 million female children enter the sex trade every year.
- Globally, up to 70% of female murder victims are killed by their male partners. In Kenya more than one woman a week was reportedly killed by her male partner. In Zambia, five women a week were killed by a male partner or family member.
- In the Russian Federation 36,000 women are beaten on a daily basis by their husband or partner.
- One in five women will be a victim of rape or attempted rape in her lifetime. One in three women is likely to be beaten, coerced into sex or otherwise abused at some point in her life. In Rwanda, up to half a million women were raped during the 1994 genocide. 71% of women in rural Ethiopia have been subjected to physical or sexual violence by intimate partners. In the USA a woman is raped every 90 seconds.
- Women do 66% of the world's work, receive 10% of the world's income and own 1% of the means of production.
- 99% of maternal deaths occur in developing countries, with women continuing to die of pregnancy-related causes at the rate of one a minute.

- It is estimated that African women and children spend 40 billion hours fetching water every year, equivalent to a year's labour for the entire workforce of France.
- Women produce up to 80% of food in developing countries, but are more likely to be hungry than men, and are often denied the right to own land.
- Up to 90% of workers in global supply chains are women.
- Globally, women make up just 17% of parliamentarians.

With statistics like this, I find it impossible to stick my head in the sand and pretend I haven't heard. This surely is not the world I thought I grew up in, only now do I realise how sheltered I have been for so many years. But here are some other facts and figures that might be easier to digest:

best places for female entrepreneurs:

The Gender Global Entrepreneurship and Development Index 2013 (GEDI 2013). Seventeen countries ranked.

US 1st
Australia 2nd
Germany 3rd
France 4th
Mexico 5th
UK 6th
South Africa 7th
China 8th
Malaysia 9th
Russia 10th
Turkey 11th
Japan 12th
Morocco 13th
Brazil 14th
Egypt 15th
India 16th
Uganda 17th

Global Innovation Index (GII) 2013. Top ten ranking following analysis of 142 countries using 84 indicators:

1. Switzerland
2. Sweden
3. United kingdom
4. Netherlands
5. United states of America
6. Finland
7. Hong Kong (China)
8. Singapore
9. Denmark
10. Ireland

UK. Department for Business Innovation and Skills, 2011

- 94% businesses in the UK employ fewer than 20 staff.
- 75% businesses are sole traders in the UK.
- SMEs (small and medium sized enterprises) accounted for more than half of employment in the UK – 58.8 %. Small enterprises accounted for 46.2% alone.

Ten shocking findings about UK attitudes to entrepreneurs and Business (May 2013: UK Attitudes to Starting a Business in 2013 – Expert Market Entrepreneur Survey – expertmarket.co.uk):

1. Men are 62.5% more likely to claim they have an entrepreneurial mind set compared to women.
2. Those under 30 are almost twice as likely as those over 50 to think they have what it takes to start a business.
3. Not having access to money was overwhelmingly cited as the biggest obstacle to starting a business.
4. Over 50% of those living in London and the South East would consider starting a business at some point in the future.
5. Women are 12x more likely to be stay at home parents than men.
6. Those under 30 are 5x more likely to say they plan to start a business in the next year compared to those over 50.

7. Fear of failing doesn't decrease (or increase) with age.
8. Those living in Scotland, Wales and Northern Ireland value being their own boss above earning more money.
9. Time is not an obstacle to those who are over 50 and starting a business.
10. Young women are more likely to be risk takers than older men.

Bank of Montreal study of 2013:

Male business owners are more likely than their female counterparts to have gotten into their role by starting their own business (65 per cent vs. 56 per cent).

Women more likely than men to have become business owners through a promotion (13% women, 7% men) or taking over the family business (21% women, 15% men).

Key factors for starting a business:

	Men	Women
Doing something they are passionate about	79%	89%
Being their own boss	78%	78%
Making money	78%	71%
The challenge of owning a business	68%	82%

Adzuna 2012 UK survey of 18-35 year olds:

Some 16% of women aspire to take home more than £100,000 a year. 20% men hope to earn this amount.

16% of women said they hoped to earn up to £30,000 a year during their career – with no plans to earn more – compared to only 12% of men.

22% of men are aiming to run their own business one day, compared to only 16% of women.

6% of men would like to become a chief executive of a company, compared to just 3% of women.

books - for your reading pile ...

Falling Upward by Richard Rohr

Feel the Fear but Do it Anyway by Susan Jeffers

Fish by Harry Paul by Stephen Lundin and John Christensen

How to Sell Clever Things to Big Companies: A Book for Everyone Who Does Clever Stuff for Businesses and Wants to Sell More of it by Carrie Bedingfield

Six Thinking Hats by Edward de Bono

Steve Jobs: The Exclusive Biography by Walter Isaacson

The B2B Lead Generation Machine by Carrie Bedingfield

The Male Factor by Shaunti Feldhahn

The Ultimate Small Business Marketing Book by Dee Blick

The XX Factor – How women are creating a new society by Alison Wolf

Why Women Don't Ask by Linda Babcock and Sara Laschever

Work with Me by Barbara Annis and John Gray

Who Moved my Cheese by Spencer Johnson and Kenneth Blanchard